In this bright and easy-to-use cookbook, you can travel the world with Priya—no passport required, just an open mind and a kitchen. Through her stories, you'll be able to see—and taste!—Greece, Mexico, France, China, Egypt, Italy, Morocco, England, India, Japan, Peru, and Trinidad and Tobago. You'll love making and tasting each kid-tested recipe—brought to life with colorful illustrations and step-by-step photos. Recipes include:

- Spanakopita
- Tostadas with Refried Beans and Squash
- Artichokes with Butter
- Crepes
- Mousse aux Chocolat
- Pork and Chive Dumplings
- Hummus bi Tehina
- Pesto Pasta
- Vegetable Tagine
- Miso Ramen
- . . . and many more!

Cooking different foods lets you learn about incredible places and cultures without needing to board a plane. With this book, the world is yours to explore—right from your own kitchen!

PRIYA'S KITCHEN ADVENTURES

PRIYA'S KITCHEN ADVENTURES

With recipes that you
(yes, you!)
can make

A COOKBOOK
FOR KIDS

These are my awesome cousins Radhika and Rishika. They're great cooks, and they helped make all the food in these photos. You'll see them throughout the book!

Priya Krishna

Photography by Mackenzie Smith Kelley
Illustrations by Anu Chouhan

An Imprint of WILLIAM MORROW

HarperCollins books may be purchased for educational, business, or sales promotional use. For information, please email the Special Markets Department at SPsales@harpercollins.com.

FIRST EDITION

Designed by **Melissa Lotfy**

Food photographs © 2024 by **Mackenzie Smith Kelley**; food styling by **Maite Aizpurua**

Illustrations © 2024 by **Anu Chouhan**

Doodles © **Shutterstock** or **The Noun Project**

Emojis: © valvectors/stock.adobe.com (page 54), © vadymstock/stock.adobe.com (page 63), © Parvin/stock.adobe.com (page 104)

Library of Congress Cataloging-in-Publication Data has been applied for.

ISBN 978-0-358-69293-5

24 25 26 27 28 IMG 10 9 8 7 6 5 4 3 2 1

RECIPE CONTRIBUTORS

Helen and Billie Bitzas, *Mia Kouppa*: Dolmades (page 13)

Seth Byrum: Baklava (page 17), Shortcut Profiteroles (page 62), Dou Sha Bao (page 83), Tiramisu (page 124)

Namiko Chen: How to Bento! (page 173), Chicken Meatballs (page 175), Zaru Soba (page 180), Miso Ramen (page 184), Salmon Onigiri (page 187)

Shanti Dev: Palakkad Shrimp Curry (page 157)

Ham El-Waylly: Hummus bi Tehina (page 94), Ful Medames (page 96), Koshari (page 98)

Tatiana Gupta: Artichokes with Butter (page 43), Gratin Dauphinois (page 45), Crepes (page 46), Quiche Lorraine (page 49), Tarte aux Pommes (page 54)

Ritu Krishna: Spanakopita (page 5), Watermelon Agua Fresca (page 36), Mom's Ribollita (page 122), Vegetable Tagine (page 135), Couscous (page 138), Dahi Bhalla, Nana Style (page 160), Shahi Toast (page 164), Salsa Criolla (page 199), Kiwicha Porridge (page 200)

Shailendra Krishna: Dad's English Breakfast (page 144)

Mourad Lahlou, *Mourad: New Moroccan*: Moroccan Mint Tea (page 139)

Rick Martínez: Pozole Verde con Pollo (page 27), Tostadas with Refried Beans and Squash (page 30), Bell Pepper and Cheese Quesadillas (page 34)

Hetty McKinnon, *To Asia, with Love*, published by Prestel: Life-Changing Udon with Soft-Boiled Egg, Hot Soy Sauce, and Black Pepper (page 177)

Ijaz Parpia: Pear and Gorgonzola Ravioli (page 109), Penne Arrabbiata (page 118), Pesto Pasta (page 120)

David Peterson: Tea Sandwiches (page 146)

Brigid Washington: Curry Chana (page 206), Stewed Fish (page 209)

Chris Ying: Pork and Chive Dumplings (page 69), "Pickled" and Stir-Fried Long Beans with Pork (page 73), Hot Pot (page 76)

Ricardo Zarate, *The Fire of Peru*: Pollo a la Brasa (page 196)

To Leena and Mona Krishna-Peterson,
my teeny kitchen adventurers forever.

CONTENTS

Introduction   x
Before You Start   xvi
A Guide to Cutting Many of the Vegetables
in This Book   xviii

FRANCE 39

Artichokes with Butter 43
Gratin Dauphinois 45
Crepes 46
Quiche Lorraine 49
Mousse au Chocolat 51
Tarte aux Pommes 54
Shortcut Profiteroles 62

GREECE 1

Spanakopita 5
Tzatziki 8
Briam 9
Dolmades 13
Baklava 17

CHINA 65

Pork and Chive Dumplings 69
"Pickled" and Stir-Fried Long
Beans with Pork 73
Hot Pot 76
Fried Rice 81
Dou Sha Bao 83

MEXICO 21

Elotes 24
Pozole Verde con Pollo 27
Tostadas with Refried Beans and
Squash 30
Bell Pepper and Cheese Quesadillas 34
Watermelon Agua Fresca 36

EGYPT 91

Hummus bi Tehina 94
Ful Medames 96
Koshari 98

ITALY 103

Sheet-Pan Panzanella 106

Pear and Gorgonzola Ravioli 109

Caprese Salad 117

Penne Arrabbiata 118

Pesto Pasta 120

Mom's Ribollita 122

Tiramisu 124

MOROCCO 129

Zaalouk with Halloumi 133

Vegetable Tagine 135

Couscous 138

Moroccan Mint Tea 139

ENGLAND 141

Dad's English Breakfast 144

Tea Sandwiches 146

Scones 148

INDIA 153

Palakkad Shrimp Curry 157

Dahi Bhalla, Nana Style 160

Shahi Toast 164

Salty or Sweet Lassi 166

JAPAN 169

How to Bento! 173

Chicken Meatballs 175

Life-Changing Udon with Soft-Boiled Egg, Hot Soy Sauce, and Black Pepper 177

Zaru Soba 180

Miso Ramen 184

Salmon Onigiri 187

PERU 193

Pollo a la Brasa 196

Salsa Criolla 199

Kiwicha Porridge 200

TRINIDAD & TOBAGO 203

Curry Chana 206

Stewed Fish 209

Acknowledgments 214

Index 215

INTRODUCTION

can't remember the first time I traveled. That's because I was a two-month-old blob seated in my mom's lap on a plane. We were headed for Madrid, Spain, a city full of colorful buildings and tapas. I'm sure the trip was amazing, but . . . I don't have much to tell you about it because, well, I was a baby!

But that's not why I'm telling this story. I'm telling it because I want you to know how much my parents loved traveling—so much so that they were willing to take not one but two crying children (my sister, Meera, was there, too; she was three) on a plane, lose all their luggage in Spain, and still look back fondly at the vacation a few months later.

My parents grew up in India; for the entirety of their kid years, they didn't know anything beyond those borders. So when we moved to Dallas, Texas, and my mom started working for the airline industry, my parents were eager to make up for lost time, even if it meant lugging around crying babies. My mom had always dreamed of having a job that allowed her to travel, and she found one that did. She spent many days on planes to the Philippines, South Africa, Australia, and everywhere in between. Working in the travel business came with perks: our family sometimes got to fly for free or at a discount if there was space on the plane. It was awesome, but also unpredictable. You see, we couldn't just hop on any flight we wanted. We could get on flights only when there were empty seats. So oftentimes we would pack our bags, maybe with a snowsuit and a pair of flip-flops, not knowing exactly which kind of climate we would end up in. Sometimes we would hit the jackpot and get on a flight to the Bahamas! Or we could find ourselves rolling our suitcases back to the airport parking lot. The only constant was my trusty

This is the actual plane ticket from my dad's first trip to America! Tickets looked way cooler back then, huh?

fanny pack, which I used to store everything from boarding passes to butter packets (hey, you never know when you might need a snack!).

All those hours spent at the airport were worth it, though. By the time I was a teenager, I had climbed inside the Pyramids of Giza in Egypt, gazed out from the top of the Eiffel Tower in France, fished for piranhas in the Amazon rainforest, and sandboarded down the hills of the Sahara Desert in Morocco. And everywhere we went, we ate. And ate. And ate and ate. Juicy, crisp-edged dumplings in China. Smooth, silky hummus in Egypt. Paper-thin crepes filled with butter and jam in France. I had grown up with Indian food: dal, rice, and sabzi. But on these trips, I was trying mostly dishes that were new to me. I'll admit, sometimes I was a little nervous to try foods that I didn't know anything about. Some of them I

didn't love, but most of them I did! With each trip, I grew more excited about eating what was unfamiliar to me.

When we got back from our trips, I knew that I couldn't re-create many of our memories—there aren't exactly pyramids to climb inside in Texas. But we could make the foods that we had eaten. My mom and I kept track of everything we ate. We would come back, learn more about the dishes we had tried, and then cook them in our kitchen. Sometimes, we'd come up with our own riffs—like sprinkling our Indian spice blends on a traditional English breakfast—but most often, we just wanted to chase these flavors we had come to adore so much.

I realized that traveling doesn't actually require boarding a plane. I could travel in my own kitchen. Cooking a dish from another country was a way of transporting me there—no passport

Introduction

xiii

required! Soon, I found tons of ways that food could lead me to adventure: Visiting a Korean grocery store in Dallas and browsing fifty kinds of kimchi. Attending a local Lunar New Year celebration, complete with a huge dragon puppet and stalls selling all kinds of noodles. Going to my friend Ethan's house for his mother's amazing Thai cooking.

Consider this book your guide to endless adventuring . . . in your kitchen! I believe cooking is one of our greatest superpowers. It allows us to travel back in time, to our memories of birthday parties and Christmas dinners and family breakfasts, and outside the

borders of where we live. You can be at a ramen shop in a subway station in Tokyo, or a roadside chaat stand in Delhi, or a cozy trattoria run by an Italian grandmother in Rome. Most importantly: cooking allows us to eat delicious things. And I am at my happiest when the food is tasty.

I want you to approach the recipes in this book with an open mind. We all have our food comfort zones. The dishes we love the most, whether that's kimchi jjigae or dal or pizza. But life is more fun when we try new things! Not familiar with an ingredient? Who cares! Cook the recipe and give it a few bites to decide if you like it. Maybe it's not for you. Or maybe you've found your new favorite dish!

Get your apron on! Cutting boards at the ready! Crush those garlic cloves! We've got kitchen adventuring to do!

BEFORE YOU START

TIPS FOR SUCCESS
(READ THIS FIRST!)

1

READ THE WHOLE RECIPE BEFORE YOU START

This will give you a chance to understand what you'll be doing next! Think of it like reading the rules before you start playing a game.

2

BE ORGANIZED

Chop your vegetables! Set your spices next to the stove! The French call this "mise en place," but it basically means getting everything (ingredients, pans, knives, and so on) together *before* you start cooking. The neater your kitchen setup, the easier it will be to cook. Timing is everything in the kitchen, and you don't want to accidentally burn an onion because you couldn't keep track of where you put your carrots.

3

KEEP THINGS CLEAN

Wash your hands frequently, and wash fruits and vegetables before cooking them. If you're working with meat, wash your hands after handling it, and use a separate cutting board.

4
LOOK OUT FOR THE SYMBOLS

These are steps that may require an adult's assistance. Don't be a kitchen zero! Ask for help when it's needed.

5
TASTE AS YOU GO

These recipes include salt measurements, but everyone has different preferences. This means that you should taste your food before serving and add more salt if you think it's needed. And don't forget that other ingredients, like olives, soy sauce, or cheese, can add salty flavors, too!

6
UNDERSTAND THE MEASUREMENTS

For the desserts, I've included two kinds of measurements: imperial (like cups and tablespoons) and metric (like grams). This is because baking is more like a science, and to get a flaky pie crust or a perfectly crumbly scone requires more precise measurements than, say, a soup or a stew. Metric measurements are more exact. If you have a kitchen scale at your house, I'd recommend trying the metric measurements. Otherwise, the imperial measurements will do you just fine.

7
KEEP AN OPEN MIND!

Try an ingredient you've never seen or smelled before! Taste a flavor combination that seems different to you! This cookbook is all about exploring all kinds of foods. Maybe you won't like all of them, but I bet you'll find a new favorite (or two, or three, or a dozen!) in these pages.

A GUIDE TO
CUTTING MANY OF THE VEGETABLES IN THIS BOOK

Chopping vegetables is one of my least favorite parts of cooking. But it has to be done! Do it neatly and safely with the help of these diagrams.

Using a knife can feel a little scary when you are first starting out. Enlist an adult to be your chopping copilot if you are still getting the hang of it.

✳ SOME IMPORTANT KNIFE ADVICE!

Which knife to use? When I was first learning to cook, I found a small serrated knife to be a good starter one: it can cut through sturdy onions, soft herbs, and even crunchy cucumbers—but it's not as heavy as those huge chef's knives, which are good for cutting through bulkier ingredients, like cabbage.

Make sure your knife is sharp. A dull knife not only won't work as well, but you'll also be more likely to hurt yourself because you'll be hacking away at your food! If your knife is not cutting smoothly, ask an adult to sharpen it using a sharpener.

Be mindful when carrying your knife. When I worked in a restaurant, I learned to always walk with the tip pointing down, and to yell "Sharp knife!" so everyone knew I was carrying a potentially dangerous object. It felt very silly to be screaming about my knife in that tiny space, but it made for a safer environment. Treat your own kitchen like a restaurant and do the same!

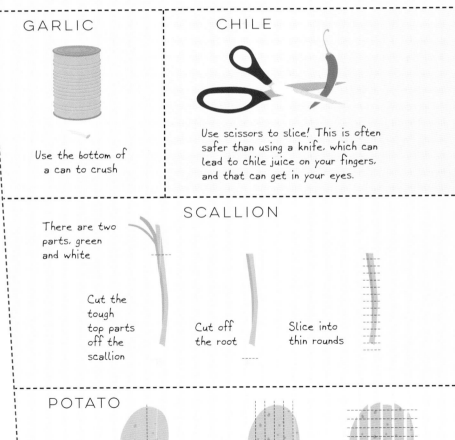

GARLIC

Use the bottom of a can to crush

CHILE

Use scissors to slice! This is often safer than using a knife, which can lead to chile juice on your fingers, and that can get in your eyes.

SCALLION

There are two parts, green and white

Cut the tough top parts off the scallion

Cut off the root

Slice into thin rounds

POTATO

Cut in half

Cut each half vertically

Cut horizontally

BELL PEPPER

  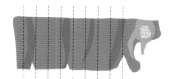 

| Cut ½ inch off the top and bottom | Cut once down the side of the pepper | Unfold into a flat piece. Remove guts and seeds. Cut into slices. | If dicing, cut in the other direction |

ONION

| Cut off the top and bottom | Cut in half | Peel | Cut each half like so | Cut across |

CUCUMBER/ZUCCHINI

| Cut off the ends | Cut in half | For half-moons, cut each half vertically | To dice, cut half-moons horizontally |

GINGER

If a recipe calls for peeling your ginger, use a spoon! It's much easier to use than a peeler.

| Cut off a piece of ginger | Cut in half | Cut each half into vertical slices | Stack the slices, then slice horizontally | Dice vertically |

EGGPLANT

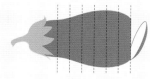

Cut into rounds and get rid of the ends

Stack rounds. Cut rounds vertically.

Cut rounds horizontally

ATHENS

GREECE

AKΡΟΠΟΛΗ
AKROPOLIS

ΕΙΣΙΤΗΡΙΟ
TICKET

My sister, Meera, and me with our friends Megha and Anjali in front of the ancient temple the Parthenon! What happened to the roof?!

My mom and me at Delphi, the site of the legendary oracle who could tell the future!

My eyes widened when we first drove around Athens, the capital of Greece, and I could see the Acropolis—high up on a hill—lit up like a movie set! Made of limestone, the Acropolis is an ancient citadel that was once the center of activity in the city. It was easily one of the coolest structures I had ever seen (why don't they make buildings with fun columns and giant statues inside anymore?). In school, I had learned about Greek mythology—which included the belief that there were gods who lived atop the highest mountain in Greece, Mount Olympus, and who meddled in the lives of humans. I thought that maybe if I squinted enough when we visited Mount Olympus, I would be able to see Zeus wielding lightning bolts or Athena, the goddess of wisdom and battle, with her shiny gold armor.

I didn't spot any gods, but every site we toured felt otherworldly. In Delphi, we visited the famous Temple of Apollo, where a legendary oracle would predict the future. We ran around the track of the stadium where the first Olympics were held. My mom has always told me it's not good to dwell in the past. But in Greece, it felt like I was living in history, and it was awesome. And did I mention that Greek food rocks?! So much deliciousness drenched in lemon and olive oil, with every meal more bright and vibrant than the last. And don't get me started on the many, many pastries filled with nuts and honey.

If you want to learn more about the cuisine of Greece, check out:

Ripe Figs: Recipes and Stories from Turkey, Greece, and Cyprus by Yasmin Khan

SPANAKOPITA

Difficulty
Level:
MEDIUM

Serves
4 to 6

Ah, spanakopita. The snack that launched my lifelong appreciation for flaky, cheesy pastry. I remember pressing my nose up against the windows of countless bakeries in Greece, eyeing those bricks of feta and spinach encased in thin, golden layers. Spinach, feta, and delicate phyllo pastry form a brilliant trio—rich, salty, briny, earthy, and buttery! There are many ways to jazz up that simple combination—this version has garlic and nutmeg. Some versions also have fresh herbs. Do what feels right!

" I like the crunchy texture. The filling was mouthwatering! I loved spreading the butter around and putting the spinach filling inside the spanakopita. I have only baked, but this is my first time cooking and I really enjoy making this recipe!

—RILEY, 7

1 cup (2 sticks) unsalted butter, plus more for brushing the baking dish

2 tablespoons olive oil

1 small white onion, finely chopped

1 (12-ounce) bag frozen spinach

2 garlic cloves, crushed (the bottom of a can works well for this)

¼ teaspoon ground nutmeg

½ teaspoon kosher salt

6 ounces feta, crumbled

1 (16-ounce) package frozen phyllo sheets, thawed overnight in the refrigerator

1 Put the butter in a small microwave-safe bowl and microwave it for 15 seconds at a time until melted. (If you don't have a microwave, put the butter in a small pot and melt it over low heat.) Set aside. You'll use this to brush the phyllo sheets later.

2 Warm the olive oil in a medium nonstick skillet over medium heat. Once the oil is hot, after about a minute, add the onion and cook, stirring occasionally, until it's soft and you can almost see through the pieces, 5 to 7 minutes. Add the spinach, garlic, nutmeg, and salt. Turn the heat up to high and cook, stirring, until the water in the spinach has mostly disappeared, about 10 minutes. First you'll see the spinach start to release water, then that water will slowly disappear.

recipe continues →

Brush the first sheet of phyllo pastry with butter.

After layering half the phyllo sheets, spread the filling on top.

Place another sheet of phyllo on top of the filling.

Brush with more butter.

Repeat with the remaining phyllo sheets.

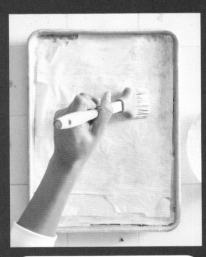

Brush the last sheet of phyllo with butter.

3 Let the onion, spinach, and garlic mixture cool to room temperature, then transfer it to a strainer. Using a large spoon, push down on this mixture a few times to release as much water as you can—this will prevent the spanakopita from being mushy! Discard the water. Transfer the spinach back into the skillet and stir in the crumbled feta.

4 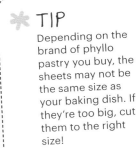 Preheat the oven to 400°F.

5 Brush butter all over the inside of a 9 × 13-inch baking dish. Carefully unroll the phyllo pastry. While you assemble your spanakopita in the next step, set a damp towel over the phyllo to keep the remaining sheets of pastry from drying out.

6 Assemble the spanakopita as follows: Set 1 sheet of phyllo pastry down in the pan, then drizzle with 1 tablespoon of the melted butter, using your fingers or a pastry brush to spread it over the entire surface. Repeat with 7 more sheets of phyllo pastry and 7 more tablespoons of melted butter. Spread the entire spinach mixture evenly over the phyllo. Place 8 more sheets of phyllo pastry on top, spreading 1 tablespoon of melted butter over each layer before adding the next one.

> ✳ TIP
> Depending on the brand of phyllo pastry you buy, the sheets may not be the same size as your baking dish. If they're too big, cut them to the right size!

7 Bake for 30 to 50 minutes, until the top is nicely browned (if the phyllo looks wet and shiny, it isn't baked through!).

8 Let the spanakopita cool on your counter for an hour, and then cut it into slabs.

The finished spanakopita will be golden brown and flaky.

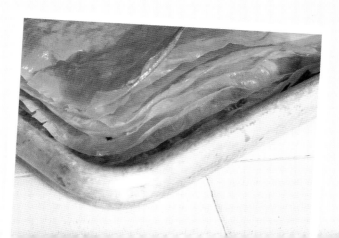

Difficulty
Level:
EASY

TZATZIKI

Serves

4

" I enjoyed grating
the cucumber,
zesting the
lemon, and mixing
the dish. Really
fun to make, and
overall a great
recipe.

—RADHIKA, 11

Before I went to Greece, I was convinced I hated cucumbers. They were flavorless! The seeds were slimy! And then I ate tzatziki, a creamy, dreamy spread where the cucumbers are enrobed in thick yogurt, herbs, and lemon zest. My mind was forever changed. Tzatziki tastes good with almost anything—it can be a sauce, a dip, a condiment, a dish eaten on its own. In Greece, I ate it with a lot of warm pita and veggies. It's also a fantastic side to grilled meat. Don't skip the step to squeeze out the water from the cucumbers; otherwise, you won't get that creamy texture!

1 large English cucumber

1 cup plain full-fat Greek yogurt

 2 tablespoons chopped fresh dill

1 large garlic clove, crushed (the bottom of a can works well for this)

¾ teaspoon kosher salt, plus more as needed

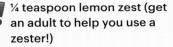 ¼ teaspoon lemon zest (get an adult to help you use a zester!)

Juice of ½ lemon (about 2 tablespoons)

Olive oil, for drizzling

1 Cut the cucumber in half lengthwise, and use a spoon to scoop out the seeds. Grate the cucumber on the largest holes of a grater (you may want to cut the cucumber halves into shorter pieces to make them easier to grate), or just place the cucumber in a food processor (with an adult to supervise!) and pulse it until it is grated.

2 Wrap the grated cucumber in a clean towel and squeeze out as much water into the sink as you can.

3 Put the cucumber, yogurt, dill, garlic, salt, lemon zest, and lemon juice in a medium bowl. Mix together, taste for salt, and add more if necessary. Drizzle the top with olive oil and serve with carrots (or other raw veggies), crackers, grilled chicken—the sky's the limit!

BRIAM

When my family went to Greece, my parents were vegetarians, and finding meatless options sometimes posed a challenge. But whenever there was briam on the menu, we knew we would be *juuust* fine. Briam is perfect for everyone; it's a simple dish that lets the naturally delicious flavors of veggies like zucchini and tomato shine—thanks to a roasty trip to the oven. Paired with some salty feta and crusty bread, it's a no-frills dinner with lots of color! The key is cutting the vegetables into similarly sized thin rounds so that they all cook at the same rate.

My mom doesn't love eggplant, which you'll often find in briam, so our briam is eggplant-less. But add it if you'd like! Also, if you have fancy olive oil—the kind that tastes like you just juiced an olive—this recipe is a great use for it.

Serves

4

❝ Me and my family really enjoyed eating it. I will definitely make it again.

—ISHAN, 9

- 1 (14.5-ounce) can whole peeled tomatoes with their juice
- ¼ cup pitted and roughly chopped kalamata olives
- 2 medium garlic cloves, crushed (the bottom of a can works well for this)
- 1 teaspoon kosher salt, plus more for sprinkling
- ½ teaspoon crushed red pepper flakes
- ½ teaspoon dried oregano

- ½ cup good olive oil, plus more for drizzling
- 1 medium red onion, sliced into thin rings
- 2 medium yellow potatoes, sliced into thin rounds
- 2 medium zucchini, sliced into thin rounds
- 5 ripe Roma tomatoes, sliced into thin rounds
- Crusty bread and feta slices, for serving

1 Preheat the oven to 375°F.

2 Pour the canned tomatoes into a medium bowl and use your hands to squish them into large chunks. Add the olives, garlic, salt, crushed red pepper, and oregano. Mix everything together with a spoon. Set aside.

recipe continues →

Greece

Drizzle a few zigzags of olive oil (not the ½ cup—that'll be used later) on the bottom of a 10-inch round baking dish. (If you don't have a 10-inch dish, an 8-inch or 9-inch dish works fine; the briam might just take a tad longer to cook.) Arrange the onions in a single overlapping layer and sprinkle them with a small pinch of salt. Then, arrange the potatoes in an overlapping pattern in a second layer, followed by another small pinch of salt; add the zucchini in another layer, with another small pinch of salt, followed by the tomatoes in another layer, with a small pinch of salt. Top with the canned tomato mixture.

 Drizzle with the ½ cup olive oil, letting the olive oil seep into the nooks and crannies of the dish.

 Bake the briam for 1 hour. To check if it is done, remove the briam from the oven, and using a fork, dig to the bottom of the pan (go from the side, so you don't mess up the presentation) to find an onion slice. It should be wilted and slightly browned. Place the briam back in the oven, preferably on the top rack, switch the oven to broil, and broil for 2 minutes, or until the top layer is browned and bubbling along the sides.

 Let the briam sit for 15 minutes before eating so the potatoes can finish cooking (don't skip this step, or the potatoes won't be fully cooked!). Serve warm with crusty bread and feta.

DOLMADES

Makes
80
to
90
dolmades

The best part about Greek food, to me, was the meze. "Meze" means "a taste" or "a bite" in Greek and refers to these fabulous spreads of snacks. One of my favorite meze is dolmades. They have different names across various countries, such as warak enab in Lebanon, but they are essentially grape leaves that have been stuffed with rice, herbs, and sometimes meat and bathed in lemon juice and olive oil. These teensy morsels are bursting with salty, tart, herby, olive oil–laced flavor—my favorite parts of Greek cuisine all in one bite.

This recipe makes a ton of dolmades, and I'll explain why! It'll take a few tries to get the rolling right, but once you get in your groove, you'll want to make a lot because it's not worth going through all these steps just to make five dolmades! Also, these keep well.

> " I liked the filling, and chopping the herbs was really fun.
>
> —ISHAN, 9

This recipe was adapted from the blog *Mia Kouppa* by Helen and Billie Bitzas.

 100 grape leaves (see the note below)

For making the filling

2 cups uncooked long-grain rice, rinsed

½ cup olive oil

 ½ cup finely chopped fresh dill

1 cup finely chopped fresh mint

½ cup finely chopped fresh parsley

10 large scallions, white and green parts, sliced

1 medium yellow onion, chopped

6 tablespoons freshly squeezed lemon juice (from about 2 lemons)

2 teaspoons kosher salt

½ teaspoon freshly ground black pepper

For cooking the dolmades

3 tablespoons olive oil

¼ teaspoon kosher salt

¼ cup freshly squeezed lemon juice (from about 1½ lemons)

1½ teaspoons all-purpose flour

Lemon wedges, for serving

✳ NOTE

Grape leaves can be found in Mediterranean/Middle Eastern grocery stores or online, and come packed in brine. Be careful when taking them out—you don't want to rip the leaves; ask an adult to help if needed.

Greece

1 Remove each grape leaf from the jar individually and open it up. As you open up the leaves, stack them, one on top of the other, on a plate.

2 **Prepare your filling.** Combine the rice, olive oil, dill, mint, parsley, scallions, onion, lemon juice, salt, and pepper in a large bowl. Mix well until thoroughly combined.

3 Now you are ready to wrap! Take a grape leaf and lay it on another plate in front of you, rib (that's the vein in the middle) side up and with the stem end pointing toward you. Drop a teaspoonful of filling near the stem end. Begin wrapping by first folding up, then folding in one side, and then the other. Once you have folded in the sides, roll the grape leaf up from bottom to top, like a burrito! You should have a tight roll. After rolling each one, examine it to ensure that you do not see any filling poking through. If you do, unwrap and reroll it. If you accidentally tear a leaf, don't discard it—you'll need it for the next step. You should have spare grape leaves left over once you're done!

4 **Cook the dolmades.** Grab a pot that is big enough to hold your dolmades—a large pot or Dutch oven will do. Add the olive oil to the bottom of the pot and line it with grape leaves. Remember those torn leaves I mentioned? You can use them here.

5 Place your dolmades in the pot, arranging them so that they are snug and each seam (aka the tip of the leaf) is facing down. I like to arrange them in rows, creating layers on top of one another. Once you are done arranging the dolmades, sprinkle them with the salt.

6 Boil water in a separate pot or kettle. You will need enough water so that the dolmades are just barely covered. As soon as the water has boiled, pour it into your pot with the dolmades.

recipe continues →

Drop a teaspoonful of filling near the stem end of a grape leaf.

Fold up the bottom of the leaf.

Fold in the sides of the leaf.

Roll up the leaf like a burrito.

Nestle the dolmades snugly in the pot.

Pour your lemon mixture over the cooked dolmades.

7 Take a plate that's slightly smaller than the diameter (the distance across a circle) of the pot, and carefully lay the plate on top of the dolmades. Cover the pot with a lid and bring to a boil. When the water has come to a boil, turn the heat down to medium-low and cook, still covered, for approximately 1 hour 15 minutes. Periodically check on your dolmades to ensure that they are still covered with water. If they are not, boil some more water and add it to the pot to cover the dolmades.

8 Check your dolmades for doneness by tasting them. They are ready when the rice is cooked and not crunchy at all. Remove from the heat. In a small bowl, mix together the lemon juice, flour, and about ½ cup cooking water from the pot. Mix well until smooth, and pour this mixture over the dolmades. Gently shake the pot so that the lemon mixture coats all the dolmades.

9 Dolmades are best served at room temperature— just remove them from the pot and transfer to a serving platter, discarding the water. Serve with lemon wedges. The dolmades will keep, covered, in the fridge for about 5 days. They can also be frozen for up to 3 months, then microwaved whenever you're craving a quick snack. Boom! You've got dolmades on hand.

 TIP
Grape leaves can be frozen for a future use by rolling them tightly together and wrapping them in plastic wrap. Place them in a freezer bag, and when you are ready to use them, thaw them overnight in the refrigerator.

BAKLAVA

My family was obsessed with baklava long before our Greece trip. Anything involving honey, nuts, spices, and sticky, flaky pastry is a yes from us. So it goes without saying that when we arrived in Greece, we were on a mission to eat as much baklava as possible. And we did. Baklava looks as good as it tastes—like gems in a treasure chest—and with store-bought phyllo dough, it's simple to make at home. Many countries, from Turkey to Iran, have their own versions of baklava. Feel free to try it with your favorite nuts and spices, and then let me know, so maybe I can come by to try some?

For the syrup

1 cup honey

½ cup packed light brown sugar

¼ teaspoon kosher salt

¼ teaspoon ground cloves

1 tablespoon freshly squeezed orange juice

1 cup (2 sticks) unsalted butter

For the nut mixture

2 cups (8 ounces) raw unsalted pistachios

2 cups (8 ounces) raw unsalted walnuts

¼ cup packed light brown sugar

1 tablespoon ground cinnamon

½ teaspoon kosher salt

¼ teaspoon ground cloves

 Zest of ½ orange (get an adult to help you use a zester!)

1 (16-ounce) package of phyllo dough, thawed overnight in the refrigerator

1   **Make the syrup.** Combine the honey, brown sugar, salt, cloves, orange juice, and ½ cup water in a small pot and set over medium heat until the sugar and salt are dissolved. Remove from the heat and set aside to cool to room temperature. You'll use this syrup to brush the top of the finished baklava.

> "It tasted really good. When we were buttering the phyllo dough sheets, I could smell the filling, and when I did I just wanted to eat half of it right on the spot. We also shared baklava with our friends and they all really liked it.
>
> —ISHAN, 9

Thanks to the blog *The Mediterranean Dish* by Suzy Karadsheh—her baklava served as the inspiration for this take by my husband, Seth.

Greece

recipe continues →

2 Put the butter in a small microwave-safe bowl and microwave it for 15 seconds at a time until melted. (If you don't have a microwave, put the butter in a small pot and melt it over low heat.) Let it cool a bit. Set aside.

3 **Make the nut mixture.** Finely chop the pistachios and walnuts by hand or use a food processor (with an adult's help!). Place them in a large bowl with the brown sugar, cinnamon, salt, cloves, and orange zest. Mix with your hands to combine and set aside.

4 To assemble, line the bottom of a 9 × 13-inch baking pan with a piece of parchment paper. Remove the phyllo from the fridge and unroll it on a cutting board. Cut it into two rectangles the size of your baking pan (depending on the brand of phyllo, you may not need to do this; it may already be the right size without cutting!) and then cover with a damp dish towel to prevent the sheets from drying out. Place one sheet of phyllo in your pan, and with a pastry brush or your fingers, coat it with a light layer of the melted butter. Lay another sheet of dough over that one and, again, brush it lightly with butter. Repeat this process with about a third of the sheets of phyllo. Don't worry if a few sheets crack here and there; some wrinkles will add to the crunchiness!

5 After laying down one-third of the phyllo and brushing it with butter, spread one-half of the nut mixture across the top and use your hands to press it into an even layer. Cover the nuts with another sheet of phyllo and lightly butter it. Continue this layering process with another third of the phyllo.

6 Spread the remaining nut mixture out and pat it into another even layer. Place another sheet of phyllo on top, butter it, and continue layering the rest of your phyllo.

7 Place the assembled baklava in the fridge for a few minutes to set, and in the meantime, preheat the oven to 350°F with a rack in the middle.

8 Once the oven is heated, remove the pan from the fridge, and with a sharp knife (get an adult to help with this!), cut diagonal lines across the uncooked baklava in each direction to create diamond-shaped pieces. You can also skip the fancy diamonds and cut it into squares! Bake until it turns a rich golden brown color, about 45 minutes.

9 Once it's fully cooked, remove the baklava from the oven and immediately use a pastry brush to brush the cooled honey syrup over the top in an even layer. It may take a few passes to use up all the syrup.

10 Let the baklava cool for at least 2 hours before serving. It keeps for a few days at room temperature and for about a week in the fridge, and it also freezes well.

MEXICO

Eyeing all the delicious fruits in the market with my sister!

I *love* shopping with my mom in new cities.

I **visited Mexico somewhat regularly with my family while**
growing up, and I even went to school there when I was fifteen. One of the benefits of living in Texas was that Mexico was always a short trip away. I loved Mexico City for its colorful streets and winding markets, and Puerto Vallarta for its beaches and seafood. I raced my sister up the pyramids of Teotihuacán, an ancient Mesoamerican city. I tasted some of the best mangoes and watermelon I had ever had in my life, and tried some fruits I had never even seen before, like prickly pear!

We essentially lived off the street food we sampled as we were walking through the city or the markets. So much of it reminded me of the Indian dishes we ate at home, with all the chiles and spices, but a lot of it felt different, too. Like pozole, a dish made both savory and a little sweet thanks to hominy—corn kernels that have been nixtamalized (more on that word soon). This chapter is an ode to street food, and a reminder that some of the best eating when you are traveling often happens outside restaurants!

If you want to learn more about the cuisine of Mexico, check out these cookbooks:

Mi Cocina by Rick Martínez
My Sweet Mexico by Fany Gerson
My Mexico City Kitchen by Gabriela Cámara

ELOTES

Serves

4

I can't think of a better way to make corn than elotes. What could be more tasty than sweet corn that's coated in smoky ancho chile powder, salty cotija cheese, and lime juice? Not much! I distinctly remember the smell of the elotes from our trips to Mexico. Just when you think, *I could eat that corn straight off the grill!* it gets doused in all these condiments that make it taste even more heavenly. In this recipe, you cook the corn by microwaving it, but I highly recommend going the extra step of charring it in a pan or on a grill for extra flavor.

4 ears corn, shucked

½ cup sour cream

½ cup mayonnaise

 ¼ cup fresh cilantro leaves, finely chopped, plus more for garnish

1 teaspoon kosher salt

¼ teaspoon ancho chile powder, plus more for garnish

1 cup crumbled cotija cheese

2 limes, cut into quarters, plus more lime wedges for serving

1 On a microwave-safe plate, microwave the corn, uncovered, for 3 to 4 minutes, until the kernels are tender and plump.

2 **Optional step:** Set a large grill pan or any heavy pan, like a cast-iron skillet, over high heat. Once it is very hot, add the corn and cook, carefully rotating it about every minute so it chars on all sides.

recipe continues →

3 Combine the sour cream, mayonnaise, cilantro, salt, and chile powder in a medium bowl. Taste the mixture. It should be flavorful but not too salty, since you are adding cheese later.

4 Place the crumbled cotija on a big plate.

5 Spritz the corn all over with lime juice and then use a spoon or a brush to lather on the sour cream–mayo mixture. Roll the ears in the cotija and sprinkle with more cilantro and more chile powder.

6 Serve with more lime wedges for squeezing.

POZOLE VERDE CON POLLO

Serves
6 to 8

There are few stews as warming and soul satisfying as pozole. Is it the brightly flavored, herbaceous broth? The soft, chewy hominy? The unlimited toppings? All of the above?! Pozole takes various forms in Mexican cuisine. Pozole verde, for example, uses fresh green chiles, while pozole rojo uses dried chiles. The key ingredient is the hominy—it's made with dried corn kernels soaked in a lye or lime solution to tenderize them (aka nixtamalization) and tastes like flavor-blasted corn! This recipe comes from my friend Rick Martínez, a pozole lover and expert. If you have extra time, simmer the pozole for a little bit longer to let those seasonings get to know one another.

" The recipe was
fun to make!
—RADHIKA, 11

2 tablespoons olive oil

 2 large poblanos, stems and seeds removed, roughly chopped

1 large bunch scallions, green and white parts separated, roughly chopped

4 garlic cloves, crushed (the bottom of a can works well for this)

1 tablespoon plus 1 teaspoon kosher salt

1 teaspoon cumin seeds

1 teaspoon coriander seeds

7 medium tomatillos, husks removed, roughly chopped

4 cups low-sodium chicken broth

2 (15-ounce) cans white hominy, drained and rinsed

1 medium bunch cilantro (stems and leaves), roughly chopped

½ rotisserie chicken, meat removed from bones, shredded (ask an adult to help with this), about 2 cups

Any combination of sliced avocado, crumbled queso fresco, tortilla chips, chopped scallions, sliced radishes, and lime wedges, for serving

Mexico

1   Warm the olive oil in a large heavy pot over medium-high heat. Add the poblanos, the white parts of the scallions, the garlic, salt, cumin, and coriander and cook, stirring occasionally, until the poblanos and scallions are just tender, 5 to 6 minutes. Your kitchen is going to smell GREAT. Add the tomatillos and continue to cook, stirring occasionally, until they are tender and beginning to brown, another 5 to 6 minutes. Turn the heat off, add the broth, and use a wooden spoon to scrape any browned bits from the bottom of the pot.

2   Carefully transfer the mixture to a blender and let cool for at least 10 minutes (this is so you don't end up with an exploding blender!). Then puree everything until completely smooth. Return the tomatillo puree to the same pot, add the hominy, and bring the mixture to a boil over high heat. Cover with a lid, turn the heat down to medium-low, and simmer until the flavors have come together, about 30 minutes.

3   Meanwhile, combine the cilantro, the green parts of the scallions, and 2 cups water in the blender (you don't need to rinse out the tomatillo puree!) and puree on medium speed until completely smooth.

4   After the pozole has been simmering for about 30 minutes, stir in the shredded chicken and the cilantro puree. Remove from the heat, cover, and let the pozole sit until the chicken is heated through.

5   Ladle the pozole into bowls and top with any combination of sliced avocado, crumbled queso fresco, tortilla chips, chopped scallions, and sliced radishes, plus lime wedges on the side.

Serves

4 to 6

TOSTADAS
WITH REFRIED BEANS
AND SQUASH

Picture this: I'm standing in the center of Mexico City's Mercado Coyoacán. The sights and sounds are amazing: chiles and dried beans in big mounds, ladies slicing coconuts with giant knives . . . and then I see it! A big yellow stand where servers in equally bright yellow shirts are whisking around tostadas piled with onions and avocado and everything from shrimp to shredded chicken to beans. I had to try this tostada! Tostadas are a party on a plate and a party in your mouth. This version comes from my friend Rick. If you don't love squash, Rick also loves sautéing chorizo—or spicy sausage—and then cooking the beans in the liquid fat left over in the pan. Yum.

3 tablespoons olive oil

 2 medium summer squash, like zucchini or yellow squash, cut into small cubes

1 teaspoon kosher salt, plus more as needed

3 garlic cloves, crushed (the bottom of a can works well for this)

1 small white onion, thinly sliced, plus more for serving

2 (15-ounce) cans black beans, drained and rinsed

1 cup low-sodium chicken broth

8 corn tostadas (you can also use hard-shell tacos, broken in half, in a pinch!)

8 ounces queso fresco or cotija cheese, crumbled

Cilantro leaves, sliced avocado, and/or hot sauce, for serving

1   Warm the olive oil in a large, deep skillet over medium-high heat. Add the squash and ½ teaspoon of the salt and cook until the squash is soft and easily pierced with a fork, 5 to 7 minutes. Transfer the squash to a plate and set aside.

2   Add the garlic and onion to the same skillet, season with the remaining ½ teaspoon salt, and cook, stirring occasionally, until the onion becomes soft and limp and begins to brown, 6 to 8 minutes. Remove from the heat.

3   Using a slotted spoon, transfer the garlic and onion mixture to a blender, leaving as much of the oil as you can in the pan. Add the beans and broth to the blender and puree on medium speed until smooth. Taste (unplug the blender before you stick a spoon into it!) and see if your beans need more salt.

4   Carefully transfer the bean puree to the skillet with the oil—I like to use a spatula to scrape all the beans out of the blender. Set the skillet over medium-high heat and bring the beans to a boil—they'll start bubbling up like a potion. This should happen almost immediately! Turn the heat down to medium and cook until the beans are very thick, like Greek yogurt, about 5 minutes.

5   Divide the tostadas among four to six plates and spread a generous layer of beans over each. Top with the squash, cheese, cilantro, avocado, hot sauce, and/or more onion—whatever you want!

BELL PEPPER AND CHEESE
QUESADILLAS

"This recipe
was easy and
delicious. It was
savory-delicious,
even though my
tongue doesn't
usually dance
when it tastes
bell pepper and
garlic.

—MADISEN, 9

It's hard to think of something that wouldn't taste good in a quesadilla.
I remember a vendor in Cuernavaca, where I attended school for a few
months, who sold only quesadillas. I loved watching him stuff the tortillas
with cheese, then put the quesadilla on a flat griddle called a comal and
smash the sides shut, the oozy cheese spilling over and forming a crispy
crust around the quesadilla. This recipe comes from my friend Rick. He
stuffs his quesadillas with bell peppers, which are sweet and crunchy. Be
generous with the cheese; otherwise, you won't get that nice cheesy crust!

2 tablespoons olive oil

 1 bell pepper, any color,
stem and seeds removed,
sliced

1 small shallot, thinly sliced

1 garlic clove, crushed (the
bottom of a can works well
for this)

1 teaspoon kosher salt

8 corn or flour tortillas

1 cup (4 ounces) grated
queso chihuahua or
Monterey Jack

Sour cream and lime
wedges, for serving

1 🔥 Warm the olive oil in a large nonstick skillet over medium
heat. Add the bell pepper, shallot, garlic, and salt and cook,
stirring occasionally, until the pepper slices are tender and
beginning to brown, 8 to 10 minutes. Transfer to a medium
bowl and keep the skillet around for the next step.

2 Working one at a time in that same skillet, toast one side of a tortilla until warm and lightly brown, flip, and sprinkle the toasted side generously with about a quarter of the cheese. Spread a quarter of the pepper mixture over the cheese and add another tortilla on top. Flip the quesadilla and toast, pressing down for extra sizzle, until the underside of the other tortilla is browned and the cheese is melted.

3 Transfer to a cutting board and cut into halves or quarters.

4 Repeat with the remaining tortillas, cheese, and bell pepper. Serve with a dollop of sour cream and lime wedges.

Serves

4

66 *The watermelon juice was wonderful! It was extremely easy to make, tasted delicious, and looked beautiful! The juice was really refreshing, and the contrast of the red juice with the bright green mint leaves was beautiful!*

—RADHIKA, 11

WATERMELON AGUA FRESCA

The reality of walking the beautiful streets of Mexico City on a summer day is . . . it gets very hot. Thankfully, the city is full of vendors selling refreshing snacks to cool you off, whether it is a raspado, or flavored ice; a mango cut like a flower and sprinkled with Tajín; or my personal favorite, agua fresca. Agua fresca is a simple juice that highlights just how awesome the fruit in Mexico is (there are also nonfruit varieties, made with flavors like hibiscus). My all-time favorite was the watermelon juice, agua de sandía. The watermelon was so sweet, and the pink color was so pretty! Feel free to experiment with other fruits. Try mango or pineapple or peach (though you may need to add some water to the blender, since those aren't as naturally watery as watermelon).

 2 cups fresh seedless watermelon cubes

½ teaspoon sugar (optional; see the instructions)

Fresh mint leaves, for garnish

1   Put the watermelon in a blender and blend on high speed until the watermelon turns to liquid, with no solid bits. If the watermelon is not very sweet, add ½ teaspoon of sugar while blending.

2   Pour into serving glasses with some ice cubes and garnish with fresh mint leaves.

FRANCE

PARIS

My sister and me with our friends Megha and Anjali. We all bought matching berets!

It was freezing in Paris! But the Eiffel Tower was incredible.

Visiting France, I fell in love with the lifestyle. All meals felt like major events. The lunches were long and luxurious. The mornings involved eating big, flaky croissants with thick lines of chocolate inside. And the dinners were always multiple courses. In Paris, the Eiffel Tower would sparkle every night, as if it were covered in fairy dust. It made the city feel like magic. In college, I lived in Toulouse, in the southwest part of the country, and I learned French and ate more cheese than I had ever had in my life. And now I try to live my life a little more French—to not hurry through meals, to make a fancy cheese plate, and to treat eating like the magical experience that it is. Let these recipes remind you of that!

If you want to learn more about the cuisine of France, check out these cookbooks:

Dinner in French by Melissa Clark
À Table by Rebekah Peppler
French Country Cooking by Mimi Thorisson

ARTICHOKES
WITH BUTTER

Serves
2

I once thought that artichokes only came in jars. In France, I learned that artichokes are a beautiful mint-green vegetable shaped like a pine cone and one of the most fun foods to eat. At many restaurants, the appetizer would be a whole steamed artichoke, often served with a tart vinaigrette (or if you asked nicely, a pot of melted butter). I love that you eat the artichoke petal by petal, scraping the soft part with your teeth. As you get closer to the heart, the artichoke "meat" gets more plentiful. My cousin Tatiana, who is from France, makes this as a quick dinner for her very awesome kids, Milo and Nina. They love to eat the artichokes with butter, but I've also included a vinaigrette recipe if that is more your style.

2 medium artichokes

Pinch of kosher salt

4 tablespoons (½ stick) unsalted butter

"Artichokes are really easy to make, and it feels fun picking the leaves off one by one!

—KAI, 9

"They are so yummy, and the best part is the heart! They are also really fun to pick off! It is a cool plant!

—ASHIYANA, 6

1   Cut the stems off the artichokes and give them a wash.

2   Add about 1½ inches of water and a pinch of salt to a large pot. Bring to a gentle boil over medium-high heat. Add the artichokes, cover, turn the heat down to medium, and cook for 20 to 30 minutes, until a leaf comes off easily when you pull it—that's when the artichokes are ready!

recipe continues →

France

43

3 Using tongs, grab the artichokes, turn them upside down in a colander, and let them drain and cool off. Scoop out the choke—the purple-tipped and usually hairy bits in the center of the artichoke—using a spoon.

4 Put the butter in a small microwave-safe bowl and microwave it for 15 seconds at a time until melted. (If you don't have a microwave, put the butter in a small pot and melt it over low heat.) Serve it alongside the artichokes.

NOTE

If you want to eat your artichokes with a vinaigrette instead of melted butter, combine 2 tablespoons olive oil, 1 teaspoon apple cider vinegar, 1 teaspoon Dijon mustard, and a pinch each of kosher salt and freshly ground black pepper in a small container. Tightly seal with a lid and shake until thoroughly mixed.

5 To eat, dip the base of each artichoke leaf into the butter and savor, using your teeth to peel the meat off the leaves. The artichoke will be more tender as you get toward the center. At the center of the artichoke is the heart, which you can eat by itself (the heart is the tastiest part, in my opinion).

GRATIN DAUPHINOIS

Serves
4 to 6

Allow me to introduce you to a way of eating potatoes that—as Zoë here can tell you—is even better than Tater Tots. In gratin dauphinois, potatoes ascend to a creamy, velvety, garlicky dimension. It is comfort food in golden, bubbling form. This recipe comes from my cousin Tatiana, who hails from the Dauphiné, the region in France where this dish is from. She likes to serve her gratin dauphinois with lamb and a salad, which is delightful. But a few nights ago, I had a late-night craving, so I ate these potatoes cold out of the fridge, and they tasted fantastic.

> " *Best potatoes I've ever had. Even better than Tater Tots!*
> —ZOË, 9

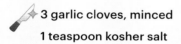 3 garlic cloves, minced

1 teaspoon kosher salt

1¼ cups heavy cream

3 medium Russet potatoes, cut into ½-inch slices

1 Preheat the oven to 350°F.

2 Combine the garlic, salt, and cream in a large measuring cup. Pour a thin layer of the cream mixture into a 9-inch round baking dish, then add a layer of potato slices with their edges overlapping halfway. Add another thin layer of the cream mixture and a layer of overlapping potatoes. Keep repeating until you have about three layers total. The cream mixture should barely submerge the last layer of potatoes. Make sure there is space at the top of the dish, as the cream bubbles up when cooking.

3 Bake for 45 minutes to an hour. The gratin is done when a butter knife easily pierces the potatoes.

France

CREPES

Serves

4 to **6**

Watching a crepe being made by a street vendor in Paris is mesmerizing. The batter gets poured onto this giant pan and then spread into a thin, perfect circle. Once it's golden brown, the vendor adds the fillings: butter and sugar, Nutella, jam, ham and cheese. Morning, afternoon, or evening, those crepes are the best thing—delicate, not too sweet, crispy with a spongy inside. You can make crepes at home, too, with some practice. It makes for a fun family breakfast. The key to a good crepe is spreading it out thin. Your first one may not be a perfect circle, but it'll still taste great. This recipe comes from my cousin Tatiana, who is French and makes crepes with her kids all the time.

2 tablespoons unsalted butter, plus more for cooking

1 cup all-purpose flour

½ teaspoon kosher salt

1¼ cups whole milk, at room temperature, plus more if needed

2 large eggs, at room temperature

Fillings of your choice, like butter, sugar, lemon, Nutella, jam, grated cheese, and sliced ham

1 Put the butter in a small microwave-safe bowl and microwave it for 15 seconds at a time until melted. (If you don't have a microwave, put the butter in a small pot and melt it over low heat.)

2 Combine the flour and salt in a medium bowl. Make a hole in the middle. In another medium bowl, whisk together the milk and eggs until incorporated. Slowly pour the milk mixture into the flour hole and whisk until the flour is incorporated. Go slowly so that the batter is smooth and not lumpy. Mix the melted butter into the batter. The batter consistency should be smooth, similar to heavy cream.

recipe continues

Swipe a stick of butter
over the hot skillet.

Ladle the batter
into the pan.

Swirl the batter to
spread it evenly.

After a few minutes,
the crepe's edges will
start to curl up.

Add your fillings.

Fold the crepe in half.

3 Warm a large nonstick skillet (about 11 inches wide) over medium heat for a few minutes, then swipe a stick of butter across the entire pan.

4 Pour ½ cup of batter into the skillet and work very quickly to spread the batter, either by gripping the handle tightly with both of your hands (be careful; you may need to use pot holders and get an adult's help!) and swirling the batter around in a circular motion, or by using a T-shaped crepe spreader (you can buy one online or in a kitchen store). Cook for a couple of minutes, until the edges start to curl up and the bottom is golden brown.

5 Add any fillings you'd like and let the crepe cook for another minute, until the inside of the crepe is set and doesn't jiggle when you move the pan. Use a spatula to fold the crepe in half (if you added cheese, make sure the cheese is melted). Slide the crepe off the skillet and onto a plate.

6 Repeat with the remaining batter, adding another swipe of butter each time—if the batter starts to thicken, add milk to thin it out as needed.

QUICHE LORRAINE

Serves
4 to 6

" I liked how easy
it was to make.
—BLAINE, 9

When I went to France, I realized that the ideal lunch is not a bowl of pasta or a really big sandwich. It is a large wedge of quiche, preferably served with a lemony salad. Quiche is so awesome—rich, cheesy, fluffy. What I love about this version, which comes from my cousin Tatiana, is the layer of ham at the bottom that functions as a salty surprise when you bite into the quiche. The amount of cheese included in this recipe may seem like a lot, but trust me, it is the right amount. Also, I love cheese.

1 store-bought pie crust (the kind that comes in a pie pan, usually found in the frozen food aisle)

2 large eggs

1 cup heavy cream

1 cup (4 ounces) grated cheddar

Pinch of ground nutmeg

Pinch of freshly ground black pepper

About 5 ounces ham slices (basically, enough to cover the bottom of a pie pan)

1   Preheat the oven to 350°F.

2 Bake the store-bought crust for 20 to 25 minutes. You don't want it to be fully baked; it's done when it's lightly golden and looks dry (it shouldn't look sweaty).

3 Meanwhile, whisk the eggs and cream together in a medium bowl until well incorporated. Add ¾ cup of the cheese, the nutmeg, and pepper.

4 Remove your pie crust from the oven and spread the ham over the bottom of the crust.

recipe continues

France

49

NOTE

If you want to make your pie crust from scratch, see page 54 for a homemade pie crust recipe.

GOT THE HANG OF IT AND WANT TO EXPLORE?

⊃→ Add some frozen peas when you add your ham.

⊃→ Want to make the quiche vegetarian? Skip the ham and add cooked vegetables. Another vegetarian option is to sauté 2 large onions and add them on top of the pie crust before you add the cream and egg mixture.

 Pour the cream and egg mixture over the ham. Sprinkle the remaining ¼ cup cheese on top and return the dish to the oven to bake for another 20 to 25 minutes, until the eggs are set and not super jiggly when you shake the quiche.

 Let the quiche cool for 15 to 30 minutes before slicing and serving.

MOUSSE AU CHOCOLAT

Serves
6

Whenever I saw mousse au chocolat on a menu in France, I ordered it. Eating a version of chocolate that tastes like whipped clouds is just a no-brainer. Each time, I was in heaven. This is a very simple chocolate mousse; it's not the most traditional way to make the dish, but it is straightforward and hard to mess up! Because there are so few ingredients in mousse au chocolat, good ingredients are key. Get the best-quality chocolate that you can find—it'll make all the difference.

> " The mousse was delicious and easy to make. I liked using the mixer to make the whipped cream.
>
> —BLAINE, 9

2 cups heavy cream

1 cup high-quality dark chocolate chips (not milk chocolate)

Thanks to Amanda Rettke, from the blog *I Am Baker*, whose chocolate mousse recipe served as the inspiration for this one.

1   Microwave ½ cup of the heavy cream and the chocolate chips in a medium microwave-safe bowl at 50 percent power for 2 minutes. Stir the mixture with a spoon so everything is melted and incorporated—it should look like chocolate sauce! (If you don't have a microwave, place the heavy cream and chocolate chips in a small saucepan and cook over low heat, stirring continuously, until they have formed a thick chocolate sauce that is steaming and just starting to bubble around the edges but is not fully boiling.) Let cool.

recipe continues

France

Keep folding until there are no white or dark brown streaks left.

! While the chocolate mixture cools, use a stand mixer or a handheld mixer (get an adult to help you) to beat the remaining 1½ cups heavy cream until it becomes whipped cream—it'll be light and fluffy, and when you dip a spoon in the cream and take it out, a peak should form.

 Add the melted chocolate mixture to a large bowl and then use a spatula to fold the whipped cream into the chocolate. This is a gentle way to add whipped cream to chocolate without losing the fluffiness. What you do is scoop the whipped cream into the bowl with the melted chocolate in as few scoops as possible, then use a rubber spatula to slice vertically down the middle of the chocolate and cream, lifting some of the cream and chocolate mixture over the rest, while moving the spatula in a wide circular motion. Make sure to get to the very bottom of the bowl to help incorporate everything.

 Keep doing this until the chocolate and whipped cream become one light brown fluffy mass with no streaks of white.

 Divide the chocolate mousse among six small containers and chill for at least 3 hours before serving.

France

Serves

6 to 8

TARTE AUX POMMES

The tart was delicious and easy to make. The middle of the tart tasted like a cheesecake. I also liked making the design on top with the apples.

—BLAINE, 9

I didn't know any French the first time I visited France, but I did learn one phrase for when I went to a bakery: "Avez-vous une tarte aux pommes?" ("Do you have an apple tart?") I had eaten plenty of American apple pies, with thick crusts and heavily spiced apples, but I loved the simplicity of the French versions I tried: an all-butter crust, thin-sliced apples, sugar, and not too much else. My cousin Tatiana hails from France, where she learned how to make an apple tart similar to this one. The tart's crevices are filled with cream, which combines with the apple juices to make this delicious goo that tastes like having ice cream inside your pie instead of on the side. This recipe includes a homemade crust, but hey, not all of us have the time to make crust from scratch. If you want to save some time, feel free to use store-bought crust. I won't tell Tatiana.

For the tart dough

½ cup (1 stick) unsalted butter, cold

1¾ cups (250 grams) all-purpose flour, plus more for dusting

1 tablespoon (15 grams) granulated sugar

1 teaspoon kosher salt

1 large egg

¼ cup (60 grams) ice-cold water

For the cream filling

1 cup (225 grams / 8 ounces) crème fraîche or mascarpone

1 large egg

¼ cup (50 grams) granulated sugar

3 tablespoons (30 grams) all-purpose flour

½ teaspoon kosher salt

½ teaspoon vanilla extract

 Zest of ½ lemon (get an adult to help you use a zester!)

For the apple mixture

4 Granny Smith apples (other options include Macintosh, Fuji, or any other tart apple)

1 teaspoon ground cinnamon

Juice of ½ lemon

3 tablespoons (45 grams) granulated sugar

1 large egg, for brushing the crust

Coarse sugar (such as Demerara or turbinado), for topping

Cream + apples = sweet, tart, apple-blasted goodness.

1   **Make the dough.** Cut the stick of butter into teeny pieces the size of peanuts. Then place the pieces in the fridge while you complete the next steps.

✻ NOTE
Homemade pie crust is great, but if you are short on time, you can always use a store-bought crust.

2 Combine the flour, sugar, and salt in a large bowl. Remove the little butter bits from the fridge and sprinkle them over the top of the flour mixture. Using your hands, quickly toss the mixture so that all the butter is coated with flour. Next, use your fingers to squeeze the butter bits into the flour mixture so that they mush into little ribbons. Do this only for about a minute or two, until the mixture starts to look like wet sand. It's okay if you still see a few larger pieces of butter here and there; this will make the dough nice and flaky!

3 Crack the egg into a small bowl and check that no loose bits of shell fell in. Then add the water and mix with a fork until the water and egg are incorporated. Set aside.

4 Finally, pour the egg and water mixture into the center of the flour and mix with your hands (or a spoon) just until it comes together and feels like cold Play-Doh. It will feel sticky at first but will firm up after a minute or two of mixing. Shape the dough into a flat disk, wrap it tightly in plastic wrap, and let it chill in the fridge for 2 hours.

5 **Make the cream filling.** Put the crème fraîche or mascarpone in a medium bowl and add the egg, sugar, flour, salt, vanilla, and lemon zest. Mix together until thoroughly combined. Set aside.

6 **Next, make the apple mixture.** Prepare your apples by peeling them and then cutting them into quarters. Carefully cut off the portions of apple core from each quarter, and then cut the remainder into thin slices, about ⅛ inch or so (the thinner the apples are sliced, the softer and juicier they become in the oven). An adult should help with this step!

recipe continues →

Use your fingers to
squeeze the butter
into the flour.

Mix together the egg
and ice-cold water.

Pour the egg mixture
into the flour.

Mix the dough with your
hands or a spoon until
it comes together.

Shape the dough into
a disk and wrap tightly
in plastic wrap.

Let the dough chill in the
fridge before rolling it out.

7   Place the apple slices in a large bowl with the cinnamon, lemon juice, and sugar. Toss them with a spoon (or your hands) until the apples are evenly coated, and then set the bowl aside. Tossing the apples in lemon juice and sugar is called "macerating" and helps them release some of their juice so you don't wind up with a watery tart.

8   Arrange the racks of your oven on the bottom and middle shelves, then preheat the oven to 425ºF.

9   **Time to assemble your tart!** Take the dough out of the fridge and let it sit for 20 minutes at room temperature. Make sure your counter is dry, and then sprinkle it generously with several tablespoons of flour. Unwrap the dough, and place it on the floured surface. Sprinkle more flour over the top. Using a rolling pin, roll out your dough into a circle 1 or 2 inches wider than an 8-inch pie pan.

10   Transfer the dough circle to an 8-inch pie pan so that the extra inch is draped over the edge. This part can be tricky, but your rolling pin can help you! Place the rolling pin at the end of the dough circle farthest away from you and then loosely roll the dough up and around the pin like a burrito. Now move your dough roll over the edge of your pie pan and unroll it across the pan. If you have any cracks or holes, it's okay; just use dough scraps and a tiny bit of water to seal them. (If there are any holes in your crust, the cream in the next step will seep through and make the bottom soggy.)

11 Pour the cream mixture into the tart shell and spread it into an even layer. Take the apple slices and lay them flat in a spiral pattern over the top, covering all of the cream. It may seem like a lot of apples, but they will fit! You'll likely have some extra juice at the bottom of your apple bowl; leave this behind so that your tart isn't too runny. Once you have laid down all the apples, very gently press them into the cream mixture.

12 Wrap the loose edges of your tart dough up and over the apples to create a border. Crack the last egg in a small bowl, whisk it, then brush it onto the crust (the visible portions of pie dough) with a pastry brush. Sprinkle the top of the dough and the apples with coarse sugar.

13 Place the assembled tart on a baking sheet, then put it on the bottom rack of your oven and bake for 20 minutes. Then adjust the temperature to 375°F (no need to wait for the temperature to come down all the way). Move the baking sheet with the tart to the middle rack and bake for another 30 to 45 minutes. You'll know the tart is done when the edges are a deep golden brown and the apples feel soft when you stick a small knife in the center.

14 Let the tart cool completely before serving. It will keep, covered, for 5 days in the refrigerator.

Combine the ingredients for the apple filling.

Mix the filling until the apples are evenly coated.

Roll out the dough on a lightly floured surface.

The dough should be a little bigger than your pie pan.

Roll up the dough over the rolling pin to help transfer it.

Unroll the dough into the pan.

60

Fit it into the pan.

Spread the cream
mixture on the crust.

Lay the apple slices
on top of the cream.

Arrange them in a
spiral pattern.

Fold the edges of the
dough over the apples.

Brush the crust with
egg and sprinkle with
coarse sugar.

Serves

4 to 6

*It did require
some patience
while trying to
make ganache, but
it was worth it;
it was delicious!!*

—RADHIKA, 11

SHORTCUT PROFITEROLES

Pastry, ice cream, and chocolate. Need I say more? The first time I saw profiteroles, they were on someone else's table at a bistro in Paris. I am the kind of person who loves to order by peeking around the dining room. Those globs of pastry-coated ice cream dripping in chocolate stopped me in my tracks. And they're just as nice to eat as they are to look at. The warm chocolate and the chilly ice cream are amazing together.

The traditional way of preparing profiteroles involves making choux pastry—a delicate, hollow pastry shell—but sometimes I want that profiterole taste in a pinch, so my husband, Seth, came up with this nontraditional but simple version using sweet rolls. Think: an ice cream sandwich with soft, fluffy sides.

For the base

2 tablespoons unsalted butter

6 sweet rolls (such as King's Hawaiian rolls), split, so you should have 12 pieces total

For the ganache

¾ cup (115 grams / 4 ounces) chopped bittersweet chocolate (or bittersweet chocolate chips)

¾ cup (180 grams) heavy cream

Vanilla ice cream (or your favorite flavor)

1 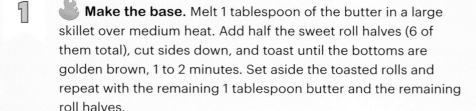 **Make the base.** Melt 1 tablespoon of the butter in a large skillet over medium heat. Add half the sweet roll halves (6 of them total), cut sides down, and toast until the bottoms are golden brown, 1 to 2 minutes. Set aside the toasted rolls and repeat with the remaining 1 tablespoon butter and the remaining roll halves.

Have you ever seen anything so beautiful?

2 Make the ganache. Place the chocolate and cream in a small saucepan and cook over low heat, stirring continuously, until they have formed a thick chocolate sauce that is steaming and just starting to bubble around the edges (but is not fully boiling).

3 When ready to assemble, lay half the sweet roll halves, toasted side up, on a plate.

4 Place a scoop of ice cream on top of each of those halves and cover them with the top halves, forming a little ice cream sandwich. Place the sandwiches on a platter. Pour the chocolate sauce over the top and serve immediately.

France

63

CHINA

The Great Wall of
China is surprisingly
steep!

Doing my very first hot pot!

If my family were a rock band, this would make a great
album cover.

As I glanced out the plane window, I could see it: this long, winding wall that went on for miles. It was the Great Wall of China, a barrier built thousands of years ago to guard against enemies. China is magnificent. We started in bustling Beijing, where I climbed a very steep—and very scary—section of the Great Wall (no wonder it scared off enemies!). Then we went to Shanghai, where skyscrapers soared upward for miles and where we bought juicy lychees from a vendor selling fruit out of a guitar case. In Shaanxi, we saw the Terra-Cotta Army, hundreds of clay soldiers created at the request of the first emperor of China and preserved over many years. And we ate our weight in dumplings, which are definitely one of the greatest foods on the planet.

If you want to learn more about the cuisine of China, check out these cookbooks:

The Chinese Kitchen and *Mastering the Art of Chinese Cooking* by Eileen Yin-Fei Lo
The Wisdom of the Chinese Kitchen by Grace Young
My Shanghai by Betty Liu

Dumplings come in all kinds of shapes and sizes!

PORK AND CHIVE
DUMPLINGS

Difficulty Level: MEDIUM

Makes about
45
dumplings

My introduction to dumplings came in the form of a dinner show in Xi'an. It included singing, dancing, and (duh) dumplings. As we watched performers in gorgeous costumes perform beautiful dances inspired by the Tang dynasty, we were served bottomless jiaozi, or dumplings, made of shrimp, water chestnut, pork, mushroom, and chicken! I was enthralled by these pillowy, steamy, chewy pockets that burst with flavor. I must have eaten a hundred. This is my ode to the endlessly varied and delicious world of dumplings, courtesy of my friend Chris Ying. He grew up spending many afternoons folding dumplings. It was a skill to be learned, a sign of love. Folding a dumpling takes some practice, but you'll get the hang of it.

" I liked the wrapper. My hand was too small, so I folded the dumplings on the table. I didn't make the regular shapes.*

—PENNY, 9

*FYI: All dumpling shapes are welcome, as long as the filling doesn't spill out!

For the filling

1 pound ground pork

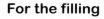 ⅓ cup minced fresh cilantro (stems and leaves)

1 tablespoon hoisin sauce or oyster sauce

2 teaspoons sugar

⅔ cup minced garlic chives (or chives, leeks, or scallions)

¾ teaspoon toasted sesame oil

2 teaspoons soy sauce

2 teaspoons fish sauce

1½ teaspoons minced fresh ginger

1 teaspoon kosher salt

45 square dumpling wrappers (the thinner, the better)

For the dipping sauce*

Soy sauce

Rice wine vinegar

Agave or sugar

* Alternatively, you can use store-bought chili crisp as a dipping sauce.

China

1 **Make the filling.** Place the pork in a large bowl and add the cilantro, hoisin, sugar, garlic chives, sesame oil, soy sauce, fish sauce, ginger, and salt. With clean hands (or better yet, hands wearing food-safe gloves), mix everything well. Really get in there and make sure the mixture is nicely incorporated and that the flavors have all been distributed properly. (Speaking of flavors, don't feel compelled to find the exact ingredients I've listed. Garlic chives can be hard to come by, for instance. Choose something oniony and green to replace them.)

2 Microwave (or cook in a pan over medium heat) a little taster portion of the filling for 30 seconds to check for seasoning. (Make sure there is no pink anywhere before you try it!) Should the filling be saltier? Sweeter? Even though we'll end up eating the dumplings with a salty dipping sauce, you still want the filling to be well seasoned, so don't skimp.

3 **Set up your folding station and start folding.** Get out a sheet pan and line it with parchment paper, then set up a little cup or bowl of clean water. I like to keep the wrappers on one side of the sheet pan and the water on the other, for reasons that will become clear in a second.

4 Orient a wrapper in your hand so that it looks like a diamond. Place 1 teaspoon to 1½ teaspoons of filling in the center. The amount of filling will depend on the size of your wrappers. You don't want filling spilling out the sides or ripping the dough. You also don't want such a small amount of filling that people think you're cheaping out on them.

recipe continues

Spoon some filling into the middle of a wrapper.

Use your finger to wet the bottom two edges with water.

Fold up the bottom corner to make a triangle.

Press to seal, eliminating any air pockets.

Fold in the two sides of the triangle.

Seal the points with a dab of water.

DUMPLING SHAPES

Some people say that dumplings were created by a Chinese doctor as a remedy for patients with frostbitten ears—hence the ear shape. Others say they're meant to resemble old coins. What do yours look like?

5 Use your finger to wet the two sides of the wrapper closest to you, then fold the bottom corner up to meet the top. You should now be holding a triangle. Press gently along the sides to seal the wrapper, doing your best not to leave any air pockets in the center. At this point, the dumpling is functionally done. You can put it on the pan, or you can show your family how much you care and continue folding the dumpling into a pretty flower shape, by bringing the two symmetrical points of the triangle together, using a dab of water to seal them.

6 To cook the dumplings, bring a pot of water to a boil over high heat, then carefully drop in as many dumplings as you like. Let the water come back to a boil, then turn the heat down to a gentle simmer (about medium or medium-low heat; there should be small bubbles). Cook until the wrappers are tender and you can nearly see through them (you can cut one open to make sure there is no pink in the filling, to double-check), 4 to 5 minutes.

7 **Make the dipping sauce.** Mix together equal parts soy sauce, rice vinegar, and agave (or sugar).

* NOTE

Dumplings freeze extremely well! Arrange any uncooked dumplings on a sheet pan (make sure they're not touching one another) and slide the pan into your freezer. Once the dumplings are completely frozen, transfer them to resealable plastic bags. They'll keep for at least a few months. The cooking process is more or less the same for frozen dumplings—it'll just take longer for the water to come back to a boil once you've dropped the dumplings in.

"PICKLED" AND STIR-FRIED
LONG BEANS WITH PORK

Serves
2

One of the most thrilling parts of eating in China was tasting all these amazing vegetables. Some were blistered in a fiery wok until the sides were crispy; others were braised until soft and slippery. And thanks to a brilliant device for serving food that looks like a DJ turntable, I could try all of them! It's hard to pick a favorite, but okay, okay, fine, I will! It was a dish from Hunan called 肉末酸豆角—a stir-fry of pickled long beans, chiles, ground pork, and garlic that is simultaneously smoky, salty, spicy, and tart. Talk about an explosion of flavors.

My friend Chris calls this dish "the greatest rice accompaniment on earth." At home in California, he doesn't always have the ingredients for the traditional version. So he came up with his own spin, using fresh long beans and a microwave.

> " *Delicious. Definitely a keeper!*
> —PENNY, 9

8 ounces ground pork

1 teaspoon kosher salt

2 teaspoons cornstarch

4 to 6 teaspoons soy sauce

2 teaspoons sugar

 8 ounces long beans (or green beans, if you can't find long beans), cut into ¼-inch pieces (1¾ cups)

¼ cup rice wine vinegar

1 tablespoon vegetable or canola oil

5 garlic cloves, crushed (the bottom of a can works well for this)

1 tablespoon minced fresh ginger

7 or 8 slices pickled jalapeño, minced (optional)

Cooked rice, for serving

China

Salty, garlicky, porky goodness.

1 Put the pork in a medium bowl and add ½ teaspoon of the salt, the cornstarch, 2 teaspoons of the soy sauce, and 1 teaspoon of the sugar. Use clean hands (or better yet, hands wearing food-safe gloves) to mix everything thoroughly. Set aside.

2 Place the long beans in a microwave-safe bowl, along with 2 more teaspoons of the soy sauce, the rice wine vinegar, the remaining ½ teaspoon salt, and the remaining 1 teaspoon sugar. Give everything a quick toss, then cover with a vented, microwave-safe lid (or just loosely cover with a microwave-safe plate so that a little steam can escape). Microwave for 1½ minutes, then carefully remove and stir. Cover again and continue microwaving for another 1½ minutes. The long beans should maintain some crunch but not be squeaky or mushy.

3 Set a large nonstick skillet or wok over medium-high heat. Once it's hot, add the oil and swirl the pan to coat. Add the pork mixture, using a wooden spoon to break it up as best you can. Stir-fry until the pork begins to brown, 3 to 4 minutes, then add the garlic and ginger. Continue to cook for another minute or two.

4 Once you can smell the ginger and garlic, add the microwaved long beans and their juices. Taste, and if the beans need salt, season with an additional 2 teaspoons soy sauce. Cook until the beans are softened but not mushy and have absorbed most of the liquid, 1 to 2 minutes max. Add the jalapeños (if you like spicy), toss, and serve with rice.

 TIP
To make the chopping go faster, pick a few beans of the same length, line them up in a stack on your cutting board, and cut them all at once.

Difficulty
Level:
MEDIUM

HOT POT

Serves
As many as you want!

> " Are we having hot pot?
>
> —RUBY, 5

I love restaurants where you get to cook your own food. I encountered one for the first time in Nanjing. We received a pot of broth, plus tons of items we could add—thinly sliced pork, mushrooms, cabbage, onions, eggs, garlic, and other seasonings. I went wild, tossing every ingredient in sight into the bubbling cauldron like I was making a magic potion. It . . . didn't taste good. The broth was too salty. The vegetables were soggy. But it taught me a lesson! The next time I had hot pot, I knew to appreciate the gentle flavor of the broth. I knew to add the ingredients that would cook the longest first, like cabbage, and the quick-cooking items, like thinly sliced meat, last.

My friend Chris, whose family is Chinese American, grew up eating hot pot at home in California; it's now one of his favorite ways to feed his kids, Ruby and Keith. This is his recipe, complete with a spread of vegetables and meat, plus noodles to finish; it also includes a delightful dipping sauce. The best thing about hot pot: it is fully customizable, so everyone gets to build their perfect meal!

EQUIPMENT

For the hot pot

There are a few different ways to set up your hot pot, depending on what equipment you have in your house.

 Skillet or pot: For a family of four, you want a 12-inch skillet or Dutch oven with sides that are about 4 inches high. You want it to be nice and heavy—cast iron, stainless steel, or thick ceramic are your best bets—so that it stays hot. A heavy pot should be handled by an adult.

 Portable stovetop, like a butane, electric, or induction burner: This will sit in the center of the table. An adult should handle the burner.

 Electric pressure cooker: If you have an electric pressure cooker like an Instant Pot, you don't need a pot or a portable stovetop. Just bring your broth to a light boil using the Sauté setting, and then keep it at the Keep Warm setting while you hot pot.

For serving

Everyone needs **chopsticks**. See the diagram below for how to use them!

Give each person a **small bowl** for sauce and a **side plate** to receive food coming out of the hot pot.

Put one chopstick between your pointer finger and thumb. When you're eating, *this* chopstick is the one to move up and down.

Put another chopstick between your pointer finger and thumb, with the middle of the chopstick resting on your ring finger.

INGREDIENTS

(approximate cook times in the pot are in parentheses)

Broth: 12 to 16 cups

This can really be any flavorful liquid of your choosing. Store-bought chicken broth works great. Vegetable broth. Dashi. Whichever you choose, opt for a low-sodium (or lightly salted) version, if you can find it. Your dipping sauce will do the heavy lifting when it comes to seasoning.

Meat and protein

Thinly sliced beef or pork (30 to 60 seconds): The best place to find thinly sliced beef and pork is an East Asian grocery store (both fresh and frozen work here). Otherwise, see if your local grocery store butcher will slice it thinly for you. Plan for about 8 ounces for adults, 2 ounces for littler kids, and somewhere in the middle for you! If you end up with too much meat, it freezes well.

Thinly sliced chicken (60 to 90 seconds): Boneless, skinless. White or dark meat, up to you. Just make sure it's thinly sliced—again, East Asian markets will have this, or ask your grocery store butcher.

Shrimp (3 minutes): Head-on shrimp have lots of flavor—add a few of those into the mix!

 Tofu (3 to 5 minutes): Go for firm tofu so it doesn't fall apart in the broth, and cut it into cubes.

Vegetables and fungi

 Napa cabbage (8 minutes): Slice into 2-inch pieces.

Spinach (1 minute): Add some greens to your hot pot!

Mushrooms (2 to 5 minutes): Enoki, shiitake, shimeji, oyster, king trumpet—all work! Tear them into bite-size pieces if they are too big.

 Taro (20 minutes): Peel with the help of an adult and cut into ½-inch slices.

Noodles

Frozen udon (3 minutes)

Mung bean noodles (2 minutes): Soak in warm water for 10 minutes before adding to the pot.

Or pick your favorite noodle: Really thin rice noodles are my personal favorite. Chris also loves ramen or shirataki.

Dipping sauce

You can go one of two routes here. Set out a bunch of different ingredients and let people make their own dipping sauce, or buy a premade version from the store. Your Asian grocery store will likely have ponzu, sesame, and chili sauces specifically for hot pot.

Or you can make your own sauce by mixing these ingredients. Feel free to modify this however you want. Don't have herbs? Skip them!

¼ cup peanut butter or tahini

1 tablespoon soy sauce

1 tablespoon rice wine vinegar

2 tablespoons sha cha jang or chili crisp/oil

1 teaspoon sugar

 1 tablespoon chopped scallions

1 tablespoon chopped fresh cilantro leaves

½ teaspoon toasted sesame oil

A few spoonfuls of hot broth from the pot to loosen it all up

1 Pour the broth into your pot and bring it to a gentle boil over medium-high heat. You don't want so much liquid that things get lost, but you don't want too little or it won't hold its temperature. About 3 inches of liquid is ideal. If you're using an electric pressure cooker like an Instant Pot, add the broth and set it to the Sauté function.

recipe continues ➡

2 Set the table with all your prepped ingredients, dishware, and chopsticks. Give everyone a sauce bowl, and put out the dipping sauce of your choice.

3 Bring the pot out to the table. If you've got a burner, set the pot on the burner and keep the heat at a simmer. (That means small bubbles! I like to start at medium heat.) If using an electric pressure cooker, keep it on the Sauté function at first, and when the broth begins to boil rapidly, switch to the Keep Warm setting until you're done.

4 Let everyone add whatever they like to the pot. Start by adding the ingredients that hold up to longer cooking: cabbage, shiitake mushrooms, taro, tofu, and so on. (See cooking times on pages 78 and 79.) Swish the meat in the broth just long enough that it cooks through. Fish an ingredient out of the pot with your chopsticks, dip it in the sauce, and enjoy.

5 If you're not using a tabletop burner or an electric pressure cooker, you'll need to bring the pot back to the stove occasionally to reheat the broth. If at any point the broth level starts to dip below a couple of inches, add more and return it to a simmer.

6 Once everyone's starting to slow down, tell them not to stuff themselves. Noodles are coming. Add the noodles to the pot, give them a couple of minutes to cook through, and finish the meal with a slurp!

✳ TIP
Once everyone's done eating, strain out any leftover meat or vegetables from the liquid. If you happen to have any leftover cooked rice in the fridge, simmer it in the strained broth to make the best rice porridge ever.

FRIED RICE

Serves
2 to 3

If you have leftover rice, you should be making fried rice! I ate version after version of this dish in China, each one with slightly different vegetables and seasonings. I love that frying rice makes the grains crispy (leftover rice makes for the crispiest fried rice!), allowing them to soak in the salty seasonings. And I especially love that you don't need a recipe for it. Just follow this blueprint, using whatever vegetables you have, and you can't go wrong.

2 teaspoons toasted sesame oil, plus more for drizzling

½ cup vegetables (cabbage, carrots, mushrooms, peas, and green beans all work!), chopped into small pieces (no need to chop peas, though)

2 to 3 garlic cloves, crushed (the bottom of a can works well for this)

2 cups cooked rice (leftovers are best)

1 or 2 large eggs (depending on how much you like eggs)

A few splashes of soy sauce

Toasted sesame seeds and chopped scallions, for garnish

1   Make sure all your ingredients are chopped, ready, and next to the stove, because this recipe moves fast! Set a wok or a deep pan over high heat. Once it's hot, add 1 teaspoon of the sesame oil and the vegetables. Cook until the vegetables are softened but still have a nice crunch, 3 to 4 minutes. (They could take longer, depending on the type and size of your vegetables: bigger pieces or denser vegetables like carrots take longer to cook than smaller or softer ones like peas.) Once the vegetables are cooked, carefully transfer them to a plate.

recipe continues ➡

China

Add the remaining 1 teaspoon sesame oil and the crushed garlic to the pan. Cook until the garlic smells very fragrant, 10 to 20 seconds. If the garlic starts to brown really fast, turn the heat down to medium-high.

 Add the cooked rice, mixing it into the garlic, and cook for another few minutes, stirring occasionally, until the rice is warmed through. Stir in the cooked vegetables, then use a spoon to make a hole in the center of the rice, and crack the eggs into it. Scramble the eggs in the hole so the yolks and the whites are incorporated, and then toss everything a few times to coat the rice. The eggs will cook as you toss them! Quickly add a few splashes of soy sauce and stir to incorporate.

 Turn the heat off, drizzle the top with a little bit of sesame oil, and sprinkle with toasted sesame seeds and some chopped scallions.

DOU SHA BAO

Eating dou sha bao is like eating a pillow. These treats are often eaten for the Lunar New Year. But why only then? When I first tried one in a restaurant in Beijing, I had never had the red bean paste it was filled with. Made with adzuki beans, red bean paste is earthy, nutty, and not too sweet. As a filling, it's like a delicious surprise. But bao can be made with a variety of fillings—if you try the red bean and don't love it, try chocolate (instructions are on page 86), or get creative.

Makes
12
buns

" The recipe was
quite fun to
make.
—NAYAN, 12

1½ teaspoons instant yeast

¾ cup (177 grams) whole milk, very warm (not burning hot, but like a Jacuzzi!), plus more if needed

2 cups (280 grams) cake flour, plus more if needed

¼ cup (50 grams) sugar

¼ teaspoon baking powder

2 tablespoons unsalted butter, very soft

¼ teaspoon toasted sesame oil

¼ teaspoon kosher salt

About ½ cup store-bought red bean paste (fine or coarse)

My husband, Seth, a big-time baker, developed this recipe, drawing inspiration from the red bean buns from the awesome blogs *Woks of Life*, *China Sichuan Food*, and *Red House Spice*. The steaming technique comes from the wonderful food writer Sarah Jampel.

1 Cut a sheet of parchment paper into twelve 2- to 3-inch squares.

2 Mix together the yeast and warm milk in a large bowl, let it sit for a few minutes, then stir until the yeast is fully dissolved in the milk. Add the flour, sugar, baking powder, butter, sesame oil, and salt and squeeze the mixture between your fingers until the dough comes together in a ball, 2 to 3 minutes.

recipe continues

China

3   Keep kneading—this means folding the dough over itself with your hands—until the dough forms a very smooth ball, which can take anywhere from a few minutes to about 10 minutes. The dough will be wet and shaggy at first, with dry bits of flour throughout, but keep kneading! It will get there! If after a few minutes the dough feels too dry, add another teaspoon or two of milk. Alternatively, if it feels too sticky, add a few teaspoons of flour.

4   Put the dough ball in a large bowl and cover with plastic wrap to let rise on the counter until doubled in size, about 1 hour. If it's cold outside, you might need some help to get the dough to rise. Boil a kettle of water, put it on the bottom rack of a *turned-off* oven, and set the dough on a higher rack to rise.

5   Once the dough has risen, place it on the counter and divide it into 12 equally sized balls (you won't need any flour to do this). With a rolling pin, gently flatten out the edges of each ball of dough, leaving a small mound in the middle so that it looks like an over-easy egg.

6   Place ½ tablespoon (1½ teaspoons) of red bean paste inside the mound of 1 of your dough portions. Wrap the edges up and over the paste and press them together to seal the dough around it. Place the finished ball seam side down on a square of parchment paper. Repeat with the remaining 11 portions of dough.

7   Once finished, transfer the dough balls on the parchment to a sheet pan and place them on the top rack of a *turned-off* oven. Turn the oven light on and place a bowl of boiled water on the rack below the buns, or on the same rack if there is space. Close the door and let the buns rise until they are puffy and have almost doubled in size, another 30 minutes.

recipe continues →

8 In the meantime, set up your steaming station. You will need a medium saucepan with high sides and a lid, a small heatproof plate, and aluminum foil. Fill the saucepan with about ½ inch of water. Next, tear three pieces of foil and crumple them into three balls the size of Ping-Pong balls. Space them evenly inside the saucepan. Balance your plate on top of the foil so it is centered inside the pot and just above the water. Cover the pan with a lid and bring the water to a gentle boil over medium heat. You can also use a steamer basket if you have one: just fill the saucepan with about 1 inch of water, set your steamer basket on top, and bring the water to a gentle boil.

9 When the buns have risen and the water is boiling, place a few buns spaced a few inches apart on the plate in your saucepan. Cover the pan with a lid and let the buns steam until they have puffed up to almost double their size and look shiny, about 10 minutes. Once they have cooked, turn off the stove and let the buns sit, covered, for another 5 minutes before removing them (this prevents them from collapsing). The buns will still be very hot, so be sure to use a spatula when taking them out of the pan. Bring the water to a boil again, adding more if necessary to bring the water level back to where it was when you started, and repeat the steaming process with the remaining buns.

HAVE FUN WITH THE FILLINGS!

▷–▷ **For chocolate buns,** place ½ cup semisweet chocolate chips in a heatproof bowl. In a separate, microwave-safe bowl, microwave 3 tablespoons heavy cream for 30 to 45 seconds, until hot but not quite boiling. Pour the hot cream over the chocolate chips, let them sit for about 1 minute, and then slowly stir until the mixture forms a smooth chocolate paste. Let the chocolate cool to room temperature, and then use in place of the red bean paste.

10 The buns taste best the day they are made, eaten while still warm.

Mix the yeast and warm milk together.

Stir until the yeast has dissolved.

Add the dry ingredients, the butter, and the sesame oil.

Squeeze the mixture between your fingers.

The dough will be wet and shaggy at first.

Keep kneading!

Knead until the dough forms a smooth ball.

After the dough has risen, divide it into 12 balls. Flatten the edges of each with a rolling pin.

Spoon some filling into the middle of the dough.

Wrap the edges up over the filling.

Wrap the other edges.

Press the edges to seal the dough.

Place the buns on parchment squares on a sheet pan.

Let the buns rise in a turned-off oven. A bowl of hot water will help them puff up.

Place three foil balls in a saucepan and set a plate on top to make a steamer.

Arrange a few buns on the plate.

Cover and steam until doubled in size and shiny.

EGYPT

We got to climb inside the pyramids and visit the rooms where Egyptian royalty were buried!

The pyramids look so epic that it's hard to believe they were built thousands of years ago!

Egypt was the trip where I realized I never wanted to stop traveling. I had never visited a country as fascinating and beautiful. It began with the Pyramids of Giza—tombs for royals designed with the precision of the fanciest building you can think of, except that they were built thousands of years ago. We traversed Egypt via the Nile River, the longest river in Africa. It guided us to the Valley of the Kings, a huge burial site for Egyptian royals, and Abu Simbel, a temple built directly into a mountain. One question kept bugging me: Where were all the ornately designed coffins that these royals were buried in? Unfortunately, not a lot of them remain in Egypt—they were taken by Western colonizers, and many of them are displayed in museums in other countries. I hope that one day, more artifacts go back to the countries they came from.

I ate so much delicious stuff in Egypt—you'll find some of it in the following pages. I highly recommend going to a market or restaurant that sells fluffy fresh pita to buy some for serving alongside these recipes. For me, eating some of these dishes without pita just feels wrong.

If you want to learn more about the cuisine of Egypt, check out:

Eat, Habibi, Eat! by Shahir Massoud

HUMMUS BI TEHINA

> " The hummus was really, really good! I really loved everything about it!
>
> —RADHIKA, 11

This is hands down the best hummus recipe I have ever prepared—and the genius comes from my friend the very talented chef Ham El-Waylly. I remember the first time I had hummus in Egypt. We went to a restaurant that had just a couple of plastic stools and an ancient-looking oven. Dough would go in, and puffy, steamy pita would come out. The pita was served alongside a large bowl of hummus with a pool of olive oil in the middle and a dusting of chile powder. This hummus recipe transports me to that little restaurant in Cairo. Ham eats this with everything from crunchy raw vegetables to shawarma to hard-boiled eggs, adding a little olive oil to perk it up every time.

2 (15-ounce) cans chickpeas (3 cups)—do not drain!

1 small white onion, halved and peeled

6 garlic cloves, peeled

½ teaspoon baking soda

½ teaspoon ground cumin

1 large pinch plus 1 teaspoon kosher salt, plus more as needed

¾ cup tahini

Juice of 2 lemons (about ½ cup), plus more as needed

¼ cup olive oil, plus more as needed and for drizzling

Smoked paprika, for garnish

Warm pita, for serving

1 Put the chickpeas (including the liquid from the cans) in a medium pot and add the onion halves, 4 of the garlic cloves, the baking soda, cumin, the large pinch of salt, and 3 cups water. Bring to a simmer over medium-high heat and cook until the chickpeas are so tender they start to fall apart, about 30 minutes. Drain using a sieve or colander and discard the large chunks of onion. Reserve the cooked chickpeas and garlic.

While the chickpeas simmer, crush the remaining 2 garlic cloves with the bottom of a can. Place them in a small bowl along with the tahini, lemon juice, and remaining 1 teaspoon salt. Whisk to combine.

  Transfer the cooked chickpeas and garlic and the tahini mixture to a food processor or blender. Let it cool for a few minutes—processing very hot food in a blender can result in explosions!

With an adult's help, blend on medium speed until smooth. Scrape down the bowl with a rubber spatula, add the olive oil, and blend again. Check for seasoning, adjusting with salt, lemon juice, and olive oil to get your dream balance. Put the hummus in a container with a tight-fitting lid and store in the refrigerator until fully cool.

 To serve, scoop the hummus into a bowl and, with a large spoon, make a shallow indentation in the middle. Fill the indentation with olive oil and sprinkle with paprika. Serve with warm pita.

FUL MEDAMES

Serves
4

When we got back from Egypt, the dish my mom couldn't get out of her mind was ful medames, a stew of electrically flavored, herby fava beans. *How did they get the beans so creamy?* she wondered. *And how does it taste so complex?* And then this recipe came to us from my chef friend Ham, whose father grew up on the outskirts of Cairo and had ful medames for breakfast (and lunch!) very often. Ham's father always braced for complaints when he made ful medames for his kids, but Ham never complained. It was that tasty. I get what he means. I could eat this all day and night. The herbs! The garlic! The olive oil! All my favorite ingredients wrapped into one dish. Warm up some aish baladi (or pillowy pita) and call it a meal!

¼ cup olive oil, plus more as needed and for serving

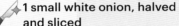 1 small white onion, halved and sliced

4 garlic cloves, crushed (the bottom of a can works well for this)

1 teaspoon ground cumin

1 teaspoon ground coriander

1 teaspoon red chile powder (such as cayenne or Kashmiri)

2 (20.5-ounce) cans fava beans, drained and rinsed (4 cups)

1 teaspoon kosher salt, plus more as needed

1 large tomato, diced

Juice of 1 lemon (about ¼ cup), plus more as needed

¼ cup roughly chopped fresh parsley leaves

Torn cilantro leaves, for garnish (optional)

Warm pita, for serving

1 Warm the olive oil in a medium pot over medium heat. Add the onion and garlic and cook, stirring regularly, until the onion is wilted and lightly brown along the edges, 5 to 10 minutes. Add the cumin, coriander, and chile powder and cook until the spices are fragrant, about 1 minute.

 Add the fava beans and 2 cups water and increase the heat to medium-high. Simmer until the water is mostly evaporated and only a little (about ½ inch) liquid remains, 10 to 15 minutes. While the beans are simmering, using a potato masher or the back of a spoon, mash them a little bit (they should retain some chunkiness). Add the salt, and taste and adjust as needed.

 Turn the heat off and mix in the tomato, lemon juice, and parsley. Taste again and adjust with more salt, lemon juice, or olive oil as needed.

 Scoop into a serving bowl and drizzle some more olive oil on top. Garnish with cilantro if you'd like. Serve with warm pita.

Egypt

KOSHARI

Serves

4 to 6

"My family all liked the tastes in this recipe.
—NORA, 13

The first time I ate koshari, I thought, *Why did it take so long for me to try this?* Combining three of my favorite ingredients (pasta, rice, lentils), drenching them in a spiced tomato sauce, and topping the whole thing with crunchy fried onions? Brilliant. This version comes from my friend Ham. His father is Egyptian, but this is actually his mother's recipe—she learned to make koshari to make his dad feel at home when they lived in Doha, Qatar. Ham told me that his parents grew up speaking different languages, so they communicated through food. Isn't that the sweetest thing ever?

A heads-up: this recipe makes a *lot* of koshari—perfect for when you're cooking for a big group. But even if you aren't, make the full batch! You can have koshari for days. And don't skip the daqqa, a spicy, vinegary sauce—it packs a punch.

For the koshari base

1½ cups uncooked medium-grain rice, like Calrose

½ cup brown lentils

2 large pinches plus ½ teaspoon kosher salt

1 cup ditalini pasta or elbow macaroni

1 tablespoon olive oil

1 (15-ounce) can chickpeas, drained and rinsed (1½ cups)

For the tomato sauce

⅓ cup olive oil

5 garlic cloves, crushed (the bottom of a can works well for this)

1 teaspoon ground cumin

1 teaspoon ground coriander

1 teaspoon red chile powder (such as cayenne or Kashmiri)

3 cups (24 ounces) canned or bottled tomato puree

½ teaspoon kosher salt

Crystal hot sauce or your favorite hot sauce (optional)

For the daqqa (optional)

⅓ cup boiling water

4 fresh Thai chiles, thinly sliced with scissors (get an adult to help with this and wash your hands after)

4 garlic cloves, sliced

1 teaspoon kosher salt

1 teaspoon ground coriander

⅓ cup white vinegar

Juice of 2 lemons (about ½ cup)

Store-bought crispy onions, for garnish

1 **Make the koshari base.** Put the rice in a medium bowl and rinse with cold water several times, draining the water each time. Once you've washed the rice, add enough water to the bowl to cover the rice by about 1 inch and let soak for 20 minutes. In the meantime, place the lentils in another medium bowl and fill with water to cover by an inch; let the lentils soak for 20 minutes, too.

2 Bring a medium pot of water to a boil, season with the 2 large pinches of salt, and cook the pasta until al dente (soft but a little chewy!), about 10 minutes or according to the package instructions. After it is cooked, drain it well and toss it with the olive oil. Set aside to cool.

3 After the rice has soaked, drain it well and transfer it to that same medium pot you used for the pasta. Add 2 cups water and the remaining ½ teaspoon salt. Cover with a lid, bring to a boil, then turn the heat down to low and cook for 20 minutes. After the rice is cooked (there shouldn't be any water left in the pot), let it rest, covered, for 10 more minutes.

4 Transfer the lentils and their soaking liquid to another medium pot and top with water so that the water level is about 2 inches above the lentils. Bring to a boil over high heat—you should see big bubbles—then turn the heat down to medium-low and cook, uncovered, until the lentils are just starting to soften, 10 minutes. Add the chickpeas and cook, uncovered, until the lentils are tender but still hold their shape, another 10 to 15 minutes. Drain the lentils and chickpeas and in a large bowl, combine the lentils, chickpeas, pasta, and rice. Toss until everything is combined. Set aside until ready to serve.

5 **Make the tomato sauce.** Wash out the pot from the lentils and set it over medium heat. Add the olive oil and heat until it is shimmering. Add the garlic and cook until it is fragrant—your kitchen should smell amazing!—and starting to brown along the edges, 1 to 2 minutes. Add the cumin, coriander, and chile powder and toast until you can really smell the spices, 30 seconds to 1 minute. Add the tomato puree and stir with a spatula until the sauce has thickened and starts to sputter a lot, about 10 minutes. Add the salt and a dash of hot sauce, if you want.

 6 **Make the daqqa (if using).** Combine the hot water, Thai chiles, garlic, salt, and coriander in a plastic container with a tight-fitting lid. Cover with the lid and let sit for 5 minutes. Add the vinegar and lemon juice and stir to combine.

7 The best way to eat this is to layer everything together. For each serving, start with a base of koshari, top with tomato sauce, sprinkle on some crispy onions, and add a dash (or more!) of daqqa on top for a little heat.

ITALY

This is the Leaning Tower of Pisa, a building that's famous for being poorly built 😂

We couldn't go to Venice without riding a gondola on the famous canals. Our gondolier even sang to us!

Pasta is one of my all-time favorite categories of food, and so when my family visited Italy, I took it as an opportunity to go on my own personal pasta tour. I knew about spaghetti marinara, but what other exciting pasta shapes and sauces would there be? I tried penne rigate, which has ridges perfect for a spicy tomato sauce (arrabbiata, page 118) to cling to; gnocchi, a soft, pillowy pasta made of potatoes; ravioli with stuffings I had never encountered before, like pear and cheese (page 109; just trust me on this); and flat, slurpable strands of linguine colored bright green with basil pesto (page 120). But there is so much more to Italy than just pasta! We visited the countryside and had hearty soups with beans and showers of olive oil and Parmesan (like ribollita, page 122). We went to Umbria, in central Italy, and had a salad made with chunks of bread and ripe tomatoes (panzanella, page 106)! And while I didn't speak Italian, I loved to sit in all the piazzas, eating a panini while my sister had her daily chocolate gelato, and listen to people around me speaking this beautiful language. One day, I hope to learn a little bit of Italian! But I know one very important word: MANGIA! Eat!

If you want to learn more about the cuisine of Italy, check out:

Essentials of Classic Italian Cooking by Marcella Hazan

SHEET-PAN PANZANELLA

Serves
4

One of my mom's favorite dinner dishes to make in the summer is panzanella, a Tuscan salad of bread, onions, and tomatoes drenched in a simple vinaigrette. The secret to panzanella is leftover or stale bread, as those pieces nicely soak up the tart oil-and-vinegar dressing. When my family finally made it to Umbria, in central Italy, one of the first dishes we made in the house where we were staying was panzanella. I loved shoveling the glistening bits of bread, thinly sliced onions, and plump tomatoes into my mouth while I peeped the colorful hills all around. This version is a little untraditional, but I like that it mixes warm roasted vegetables with cold cucumbers and plenty of cheese and fresh herbs.

2 cups sourdough bread, torn into bite-size pieces (stale bread works best here!)

1 cup cherry tomatoes

1 small red onion, sliced

1 small red bell pepper, stem and seeds removed, sliced

1 small yellow bell pepper, stem and seeds removed, sliced

3 tablespoons plus 1½ teaspoons olive oil

1½ teaspoons kosher salt

1¼ teaspoons freshly ground black pepper

2 tablespoons red wine vinegar

1 teaspoon honey

Juice of ½ lemon (about 2 tablespoons)

¼ cup pitted and halved kalamata olives

2 Persian cucumbers or ½ English cucumber, diced

2 tablespoons torn fresh basil leaves

2 ounces feta, crumbled

1   Preheat the oven to 425ºF.

2   Place the bread, tomatoes, onion, and bell peppers on a sheet pan. Drizzle with 3 tablespoons of the olive oil and toss to coat. Season with 1 teaspoon of the salt and 1 teaspoon of the black pepper. Roast until the veggies are shriveled and just starting to blister a little, about 20 minutes.

3   Meanwhile, make the dressing. Combine the vinegar, honey, lemon juice, and the remaining 1½ teaspoons olive oil, ½ teaspoon salt, and ¼ teaspoon black pepper in a jar, cover tightly, and shake until emulsified (a fancy term that just means it's all incorporated into a thick dressing).

4   When the veggies are done, scatter the olives, cucumbers, and basil leaves on top. Drizzle with the dressing, top with the feta, and serve.

PEAR AND GORGONZOLA
RAVIOLI

Do you remember that scene in the movie *Ratatouille* when Remy the rat bites into a strawberry and then a piece of cheese and realizes that when you mix sweet with salty, it makes a brand-new flavor that tastes even better than the individual ingredients? That's how I felt when I tried pear and gorgonzola together. We were at a restaurant called La Giostra in Florence—a cozy spot where you feel like you are at someone's grandmother's house. This pear and gorgonzola ravioli was a flavor symphony. The pear balanced out the salty, funky cheese. This recipe—which comes to us from my parents' friend Ijaz Parpia, who lived in Italy for a number of years while growing up—is an ode to that dish. It's also a great way to dip your toes into the world of making pasta from scratch, without needing a pasta maker.

Serves
4

" *My brother and grandparents thought it was yummy.*
—ASHIYANA, 6

For the filling

8 ounces whole-milk ricotta (about 1 cup)

2 tablespoons unsalted butter

 1½ ripe Bartlett pears, peeled and diced

4 ounces gorgonzola, crumbled (about ½ cup)

1 tablespoon chopped fresh sage leaves

For the pasta

1 cup semolina flour, plus more for dusting

½ teaspoon kosher salt

1 tablespoon olive oil

½ cup cold water

For cooking/saucing the pasta

3 tablespoons kosher salt

3 tablespoons unsalted butter, cut into slices

10 fresh sage leaves

VARIATION

▷→ If you don't like gorgonzola, just swap the gorgonzola in the recipe for more ricotta and add a pinch of salt.

 NOTE

Semolina flour is made from durum wheat; it has a slightly sweet and nutty flavor, a coarse texture, and a pretty pale-yellow color. It makes for very flavorful pasta! You can find it at most grocery stores or order it online.

Italy

1 **Make the filling.** Line a colander with several overlapping paper towels and set it over a plate. Add the ricotta to the colander and let it drain for 30 minutes. Discard the liquid that strains out, reserving the ricotta.

2 Melt the butter in a large skillet over medium heat, then turn the heat down to medium-low and add the pears. Cook until you can easily smush the pears with a spoon, a few minutes. Turn the heat down to low, add the gorgonzola, and continue to cook until the cheese melts into the pear mixture, 1 to 2 minutes. Stir in the ricotta and turn off the heat. Mix in the chopped sage. Transfer the filling to a bowl and refrigerate for at least 30 minutes to make the ravioli easier to fill.

3 **Make the pasta.** Mix together the flour, salt, and olive oil in a medium bowl—the mixture should feel like wet sand. Dump the flour mixture onto the counter in a pile, make a well in the center with one hand, then add a little of the water into the well and use your other hand to incorporate it into the dough, moving the flour from the outside into the water in the center.

4 Keep making a well, adding a little water to the middle, and then incorporating it into the dough from the outside to the inside. Once the dough comes together into a smooth and soft ball, without any dough pieces falling off, stop adding water— you may not need the full ½ cup!

5 Knead the dough for 10 to 15 minutes, until it is smoother and, more importantly, very soft and stretchy (like Play-Doh). This basically means throwing it on the table and folding it over itself with your hands. Wrap the dough in plastic wrap and let it rest for 20 minutes (do not refrigerate).

6 Use semolina flour to lightly dust a clean working surface, like a kitchen counter or a large cutting board. Use a rolling pin to roll the dough out into a 13 × 20-inch rectangle—it doesn't have to be super precise (the edges can be rounded). This may take a little muscle and an adult's help! You want it to feel as thin as a bedsheet.

recipe continues →

Italy

7 Sprinkle more semolina flour onto the dough rectangle and cut it lengthwise into 6 strips, each one a little wider than 2 inches. Dollop ½ tablespoon (1½ teaspoons) of filling onto 3 of the strips, about 2 inches apart (you should be able to get 6 to 8 dollops per strip).

8 Fill a bowl with warm water and use your finger to outline the edges of the filling-covered strips with water (this will help the dough stick). Place one of the strips without filling on top of a strip with filling and use your fingers to seal the dough around the filling, stretching it as necessary but being careful not to break the dough. Use a knife to cut the ravioli into pieces, and then use a fork to crimp the edges to further seal them. Make sure you seal the edges tightly; otherwise, air bubbles will form and the ravioli won't cook nicely.

9 Toss the finished ravioli in a little more semolina flour (so they don't stick to one another) and arrange on a sheet pan or plate.

10 **Cook the pasta.** Fill a large pot a little over halfway with water and bring it to a boil. Once the water is boiling, add the salt. Add the ravioli to the water and cook until the ravioli rise to the top, 2 to 3 minutes. Use a slotted spoon to transfer the ravioli to a platter.

11 **Make the sauce.** Melt the butter slices in a small pan over medium heat. Cook, stirring regularly, until the butter starts to look brown, 5 to 8 minutes. Add the sage leaves and cook until the leaves are crisp. Drizzle this mix onto the ravioli and serve immediately.

 TIP
If you don't want to make the ravioli from scratch, you can also use the filling as a sauce for store-bought pasta—just boil 8 ounces of your favorite pasta, and toss it with the sauce, using a few splashes of the pasta cooking water to help the sauce cling to the pasta.

Mix together the flour, salt, and olive oil.

The mixture should feel like wet sand.

Dump the flour mixture onto the counter.

Make a well in the center.

Add a little water.

Push the flour from the edges into the center to mix the dough.

Add more water . . .

. . . and keep mixing.

Keep adding water and mixing.

Knead until you have a smooth, soft ball. Cover the dough in plastic wrap and let rest for 20 minutes.

Roll out the dough on a lightly floured surface.

Roll it into a very thin rectangle.

Cut the rectangle
into 6 long strips.

Dollop filling onto
3 of the strips and, using
your fingers, outline those
strips with water.

Top with the other
3 strips and press around
the filling to seal.

Cut the ravioli into pieces.

Crimp the edges of each
ravioli with a fork.

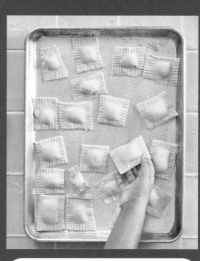

Toss the ravioli in
semolina flour so they
don't stick together.

CAPRESE SALAD

Serves
4

Caprese salad screams Italy. Why? For one, it looks like the Italian flag, with its red (tomato), white (mozzarella), and green (basil). The key to a good caprese is excellent ingredients and, in particular, the best mozzarella you can get your hands on! In Italy, we visited a town known across the country for its mozzarella di bufala, aka mozzarella made with water buffalo milk. I was used to the mozzarella that comes as string cheese, but this mozzarella was creamy and bouncy. You can get great mozzarella outside Italy now, and you can make this simple salad by pairing the cheese with sliced juicy tomatoes, basil leaves, and a generous drizzle of olive oil.

1 (8-ounce) ball fresh mozzarella

1 large tomato

8 to 10 fresh basil leaves

Olive oil, for drizzling

Kosher salt and freshly ground black pepper

1   Slice the mozzarella into ½-inch medallions (think: as thick as your pinky). Cut the tomato into slices of the same thickness.

2   On a platter, arrange the mozzarella and tomato slices in alternating rows. Tear the basil leaves and scatter them over the top. Drizzle the whole thing with olive oil so that each piece of tomato and mozzarella gets a nice splash! Sprinkle the salad with salt and pepper.

Serves

2

PENNE ARRABBIATA

My family's first night in Italy, it was rainy and dark, and we were so hungry. On this tiny street in Rome, we stumbled across an even tinier restaurant with a handwritten menu and a friendly owner who immediately started welcoming us in his rapid Italian. We didn't understand a word! But we had a hunch this guy's food would be awesome. We were right. He made a mean penne arrabbiata. Arrabbiata has all the best parts of a great tomato sauce—salty, sweet, juicy—but kicked up a notch with spice (but not too spicy!). This recipe comes from my parents' friend Ijaz, who lived in Italy as a child and is an amazing cook. When I was growing up, my family made penne arrabbiata once a week. Spicy pastas are my jam.

3 tablespoons olive oil

1 garlic clove, crushed (the bottom of a can works well for this)

1 (14.5-ounce) can crushed tomatoes

 1 tablespoon chopped fresh basil leaves

1 teaspoon crushed red pepper flakes

8 ounces penne rigate (the kind with ridges)

⅓ cup grated Parmesan, plus more for serving

1   Warm the olive oil in a large skillet over medium heat for about 1 minute. Add the garlic and let it cook for another minute, until you can really smell it. Add the tomatoes, basil, and crushed red pepper flakes. Turn the heat down to low, and cook for 10 to 15 minutes.

Meanwhile, cook the pasta according to the package instructions, cooking it for 1 minute less than it says to on the package because it will get cooked more when added to the sauce.

Once the pasta is cooked, scoop out ⅓ cup of the pasta water and then drain the rest. Add the reserved pasta water to the sauce and stir to incorporate. Add the drained pasta to the sauce. Add the Parmesan to the pasta and toss so the cheese becomes part of the sauce.

Divide the pasta between two bowls and sprinkle with more Parmesan.

PESTO PASTA

Serves

2

Pesto is, in my opinion, a perfect sauce—it's got freshness from the herbs, umami (a Japanese word for flavors that are savory and craveable!) from the cheese, and richness from the olive oil, with a little kick from the garlic. Basil is the classic herb to make pesto with, but I've also tried it with parsley! Mint! Arugula! When we went to Italy, I was on a mission to find the best pesto pasta. While pesto comes from Genoa, I probably tried it in every city we visited, from Venice to Pisa to Florence to Rome. Which one was the best? I couldn't say. I liked them all. Special thanks to my parents' friend Ijaz, who developed this pesto recipe.

> "The pesto was perfectly balanced, and it was the right amount of salt, tang, and flavor!
>
> —RADHIKA, 11

¼ cup olive oil, plus more for drizzling

¼ cup pine nuts

1 garlic clove, peeled

½ teaspoon kosher salt

2 cups fresh basil leaves

½ cup grated Parmesan

Freshly squeezed lime juice

8 ounces pasta
(I recommend fusilli)

1 Put the olive oil, pine nuts, garlic, and salt in a blender and blend on the lowest setting until everything is thoroughly combined, about 1½ minutes. Add the basil and blend on low speed again until the basil leaves are incorporated; they should look like small flecks. (You may have to scrape down the sides with a spatula every so often to keep blending; make sure you ask an adult to help with this.)

2 Add the Parmesan and blend again on low speed until the cheese is incorporated, about a minute. Transfer to a bowl and add a spritz of lime to keep the pesto from turning black.

3 Cook the pasta according to the package instructions, drain, and let it cool to nearly room temperature. Drizzle some olive oil on the pasta and toss until it looks glossy. Add the pesto and toss again to coat; the pasta should turn green!

Difficulty
Level:
MEDIUM

MOM'S RIBOLLITA

Serves

4

I always thought pasta was the best thing that Italy had to offer, and then I tried ribollita—a hearty bean soup that is the food equivalent of a big hug. We were in Tuscany, having dinner at a tiny farmhouse. Our surroundings were goats and cows. Deep bowls of ribollita appeared before us, each one with a shower of Parmesan and a shiny pool of olive oil. When we got back home to Texas, my mom couldn't stop thinking about this dish, so she made her own take, with more veggies, olives to garnish, and black peppercorns for a little kick. A version of this recipe appears in my cookbook *Indian-ish*, and it was too good not to share here. In my opinion, there is no limit to how much Parmesan you can grate on top of this soup. I say the more cheese, the better!

¼ cup olive oil, plus more for serving

1 teaspoon whole black peppercorns

 1 medium yellow onion, finely diced

1 medium zucchini, diced into ½-inch pieces

2 medium Roma tomatoes, diced into ½-inch pieces

2 (15-ounce) cans cannellini or great northern beans, drained and rinsed

1 tablespoon fresh rosemary, torn into small pieces, plus more for serving

2 garlic cloves, crushed (the bottom of a can works well for this)

1 teaspoon kosher salt, plus more as needed

1 teaspoon freshly ground black pepper

1 cup sourdough bread, torn into ½-inch pieces (stale bread works best here!)

Pitted kalamata olives, chopped, for garnish

Shaved or grated Parmesan, for garnish

1   Warm the olive oil in a large pot or Dutch oven over medium-low heat. When the oil gets hot and begins to shimmer, add the peppercorns. Cook, stirring, until you can smell the peppercorns, about a minute, then increase the heat to medium-high and add the onions. Cook until the onions become pale and soft, 5 to 7 minutes. Turn the heat down to medium, add the zucchini and tomatoes, and cook until the zucchini has softened but is still bright green in color, 8 to 10 minutes.

2   Add the beans, rosemary, garlic, salt, ground black pepper, and 4 cups water. Increase the heat to high and bring the soup to a boil. Then turn the heat down to low, mash the beans lightly with a potato masher or a large spoon (*juuust* so they soak into the soup—you still want them to keep most of their shape), cover, and cook for 10 minutes. Right at the end of the cooking time, stir in the bread. Taste and add more salt if necessary—*but* remember that you'll also be adding olives and cheese, which are both salty.

3   To serve, ladle the soup into individual bowls and garnish with more rosemary, the olives, Parmesan, and a drizzle of olive oil.

TIRAMISU

Serves

6 to 8

> The recipe and the construction of the tiramisu was fun.
>
> —NAYAN, 12

Thanks to my husband, Seth, for this recipe. He took inspiration from Lily Ernst, from the blog *Little Sweet Baker*, and Marzia Aziz, from *Little Spice Jar*.

Remember that tiny restaurant that looked like a grandma's house from page 109, the one where I had the amazing ravioli? I didn't mention dessert. On the menu it was listed as "Tiramisu-su-su-su." I'm still not sure why! I wasn't even sure that I liked tiramisu. But I ordered it based on how fluffy and beautifully cocoa-dusted it looked on another diner's table, and I'm glad I did. That one experience kicked off a lifelong love of tiramisu—a creamy dessert that's as close to a chocolate cloud as it gets. If you don't think you'll like a dessert with coffee in it, think again. The coffee supercharges the chocolate flavor.

For the syrup

1 cup (240 grams) strong brewed coffee, hot (ask an adult to help make the coffee!)

1 teaspoon vanilla extract

2 tablespoons granulated sugar

1 tablespoon cocoa powder

For the filling and assembly

2 cups (453 grams / 16 ounces) mascarpone, at room temperature

1½ teaspoons vanilla extract

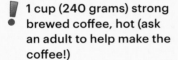 Zest of ½ lemon (get an adult to help you use a zester!)

½ teaspoon kosher salt

1 cup (135 grams) powdered sugar

1½ cups (360 grams) heavy cream

About 30 ladyfinger cookies (look for the crispy kind, not the soft, spongy kind)

1½ teaspoons cocoa powder, or 1 ounce of your favorite bar of dark chocolate (74% cacao or so)

1 **Make the syrup.** Whisk together the hot coffee, vanilla, granulated sugar, and cocoa powder in a medium bowl until the liquid is smooth and the sugar has dissolved. Put it in the refrigerator to cool.

recipe continues

Look at those layers!

2 ! **Make the filling.** Put the mascarpone in a large bowl and add the vanilla, lemon zest, salt, and powdered sugar. Using a handheld mixer (get an adult to help you with this), mix on low speed for about 30 seconds so that the sugar doesn't fly all over the kitchen. Scrape down the sides of your bowl with a rubber spatula and then increase the mixer speed to high and whip until the cheese is lighter and fluffier, about a minute. (For this step, you can also use a stand mixer fitted with the whisk attachment.)

3 Next, add the heavy cream to the cheese mixture and blend on the lowest speed until the mixture starts to look smooth, about 30 seconds. Scrape down the sides of your bowl to make sure there are no bits of cheese or sugar that haven't been incorporated. Then whip on high speed until the mixture is light, fluffy, and stiff, 1 or 2 more minutes.

4 **Assemble the tiramisu.** You'll need an 8-inch square pan (a pie pan or small casserole dish of about the same size would also work). Have your pan, ladyfingers, coffee syrup, and cheese mixture ready. Tightly and evenly line the bottom of the pan with about half of your ladyfingers. Spoon an even coating of the coffee syrup over the cookies, using half of the mixture. It might seem like a lot of liquid, but the cookies will act like little sponges, so don't hold back.

5 Next, spread half of your cheese mixture over the cookies with a big spoon or spatula, covering them completely with an even layer.

6 Repeat with the remaining cookies and cheese mixture, lining the pan with the rest of the cookies, soaking them with the remaining coffee syrup, and then covering them with the remaining cheese mixture. Smooth the top with your spoon or spatula as best as you can.

7 ! To finish the tiramisu, sprinkle the top with either the cocoa powder or dark chocolate. If using cocoa powder, a small sieve or tea strainer is a helpful tool to dust the dessert evenly with powder. If using chocolate, use a cheese grater to grate the bar over the top (get an adult to help with this).

8 Let the tiramisu set in the refrigerator for at least 3 to 4 hours before serving. It will keep in the refrigerator for about 3 days.

Arrange half of the ladyfingers in the pan.

Spoon coffee syrup over the cookies.

Spread half of the cheese mixture over the cookies.

Add the rest of the cookies and soak with more coffee syrup.

Spread the rest of the cheese mixture on top.

Sprinkle with cocoa powder or dark chocolate.

MOROCCO

Hanging with my friend Megha at the colorful markets! Our moms bought
a lot of pottery.

My family with our best friends, the Motgis, after spending all
day playing in the sands of the Sahara Desert.

What excited me so much about Morocco (besides the camel ride—did you know camels have a lot of boogers?) was how in a single country, there were so many different landscapes. One day, we were in the medina, a winding marketplace full of narrow alleyways where vendors sold colorful rugs and beautiful leather sandals. It was like being in a maze! Another day, we were in the High Atlas Mountains, where the skies were so clear and blue and vast that I wanted to shout into the abyss, "I'm the queen of the *woooooorld*!" (I did not, and I regret it.) And then there was the desert. Miles upon miles of silky soft sand that we spent hours rolling in and sliding down. I am so excited to visit Morocco again one day soon; until then, I'll keep cooking all this delicious Moroccan food—nutty-tasting couscous and hearty vegetable tagines and minty teas—and reliving the memories.

If you want to learn more about the cuisine of Morocco, check out these cookbooks:

Mourad: New Moroccan by Mourad Lahlou
Arabesque: A Taste of Morocco, Turkey, and Lebanon by Claudia Roden

ZAALOUK
WITH HALLOUMI

Serves
2 to 4

Give me zaalouk any day of the week! Hot, cold, with pita, with a salad. This dish can truly do it all. I think the first time I tried this in Morocco, I did a little dance because the combination of hot, salty cheese and silky eggplant and tomatoes made my taste buds sing. With just a few herbs and spices, you get big flavors. If you don't love halloumi, you could very easily swap it out for a different kind of cheese, like paneer or provolone. Just be careful when you are frying the cheese, and keep plenty of distance from the pan—hot oil on your hands is no fun.

"Liked it a lot.
—MILO, 6

2 tablespoons olive oil

2 garlic cloves, crushed (the bottom of a can works well for this)

2 teaspoons cumin seeds

 1 large eggplant, cut into cubes

1 teaspoon kosher salt

1 (14.5-ounce) can crushed tomatoes

½ cup roughly chopped fresh parsley leaves

¼ cup roughly chopped fresh cilantro leaves

1 teaspoon smoked paprika

Juice of ½ lemon (about 2 tablespoons)

10 ounces halloumi, cut into ½-inch slices

Crusty bread, for serving

Morocco

133

1 Warm 1 tablespoon of the olive oil in a large skillet over medium-high heat. Add the garlic, and once you can really smell it—after 30 seconds to a minute—add the cumin seeds. Toast the cumin seeds until they turn a darker shade of brown and become very fragrant, another minute or so (you should be able to really smell their smokiness!). Add the eggplant and salt and spread the eggplant into one layer in the pan. Let the eggplant cook without stirring for about 5 minutes—it'll develop a golden-brownish crust. Then add the tomatoes, parsley, cilantro, and paprika. Turn the heat down to medium-low and cook, uncovered, for 10 to 14 minutes, mashing the mixture with a potato masher or the back of a large spoon as it simmers. It should look like a chunky sauce, and the eggplant should be nice and soft. Remove from the heat and stir in the lemon juice.

2 In another large skillet, warm the remaining 1 tablespoon olive oil over medium-high heat. Once the oil is hot, nestle the halloumi slices in the pan, and let them cook until the underside is golden, 2 to 3 minutes. Flip and repeat to get that other side golden, another 2 to 3 minutes. Be careful when flipping, as the oil will be hot! Get an adult's help. I like to use tongs for this.

3 Serve the zaalouk with the pan-fried halloumi and your favorite crusty bread.

VEGETABLE TAGINE

Difficulty Level: MEDIUM

Serves
4

When we went to Morocco, we traveled all across the country. But we always ate tagine, a stew of chickpeas and vegetables simmered in a flavorful bath of spices and often served over couscous (page 138). It would come in a colorful, ornately decorated wide bowl with a lid that looks like a circus tent (the serving dish is also called a tagine!). When the lid was lifted, the warming scent of the stew would hit my nostrils and make me even hungrier. I had tagine with different combinations of vegetables, or dried fruits (like prunes and apricots), or harissa (a type of chili paste—very yummy). This recipe has a lot of spices, but they all play important roles.

> " There were a lot of new spices that I have never cooked with. The recipe had lots of new flavors that I liked.
>
> —ISHAN, 9

For the spice blend

¼ teaspoon ground cloves

¼ teaspoon ground ginger

¼ teaspoon ground allspice

½ teaspoon paprika

½ teaspoon turmeric

½ teaspoon ground fennel seeds

½ teaspoon ground cumin

For the tagine

3 tablespoons olive oil

 ½ small yellow onion, diced

2 Roma tomatoes, diced

1 cup medium-diced butternut squash (best to buy this already diced from the grocery store, or get an adult to cut the squash for you; no need to peel)

1 small yellow potato, diced

2 medium carrots, sliced into rounds

1 teaspoon kosher salt, plus more as needed

1 (15-ounce) can chickpeas, drained and rinsed

3 or 4 slices lemon, plus juice of ½ lemon (about 2 tablespoons)

¼ cup pitted and roughly chopped olives (a mix of kalamata and green is best)

½ teaspoon saffron threads

Couscous (page 138), for serving

✳ NOTE
Saffron adds a lot of flavor here, but it is expensive. You can make the recipe without it and the dish will still taste wonderful.

1 **Make the spice blend.** In a small bowl, mix together the cloves, ginger, allspice, paprika, turmeric, fennel, and cumin (all the spices *except* the saffron).

2 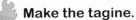 **Make the tagine.** Warm the olive oil in a medium Dutch oven or other pot over medium heat. Add the onions and cook, stirring occasionally, until they are golden brown along the edges, 8 to 10 minutes. Add the tomatoes and cook until they start to soften, 1 to 2 minutes. Add the spice mix from the bowl (but not the saffron yet!). Let the spices cook until they are really filling your kitchen with nice smells, 2 to 3 minutes.

3 Add the squash, potato, carrots, salt, and 2 cups water. Cover and cook until the potato and carrots are soft and you can pierce them with a fork, 5 to 7 minutes. Add the chickpeas, 1 more cup water, the lemon slices, and the olives. Cover and cook until the broth has thickened and you can really taste the flavors (get in there with a spoon and try it!), another 5 to 10 minutes. Uncover and mix everything well. Mash the potatoes a little bit with the back of a large spoon. Taste and adjust the salt, if necessary. Remove from the heat and mix in the lemon juice.

4 Combine the saffron threads and 2 tablespoons water in a small bowl and mash the threads using the back of the spoon—the water should turn golden. Add the saffron mixture to the tagine and mix well. Transfer to a serving dish and serve with couscous.

COUSCOUS

Serves

4

"Mixing it was fun, waiting was not.
—ISHAN, 9

You can't have tagine (page 135) without couscous! A fun fact is that while couscous may look like a grain, it's actually a pasta. That said, I've always thought couscous combines the best parts of a grain and a pasta—it's hearty and filling, and it soaks up sauce well. Also, it takes very little effort to make! It was a staple of many of the meals we ate in Morocco, and I loved that it wasn't always served plain—it was often fragrant with spices. This version has cumin, which is smoky and complex, and goes especially well with the fruity flavor of the olive oil. This is couscous good enough to eat by itself!

1 cup couscous

½ teaspoon kosher salt

1 teaspoon cumin seeds

2 tablespoons olive oil

1 Bring 2 cups water to a boil in a medium pot over high heat. Once the water is boiling rapidly (you'll see lots of big bubbles), add the couscous, salt, and cumin seeds. Mix well, and once the water is boiling again, turn off the heat, cover the pot with a lid, and let sit for about 30 minutes.

2 After 30 minutes, lift the lid, fluff up the couscous with a fork, and stir in the olive oil.

MOROCCAN MINT TEA

Serves
2 to 4

Adapted from
Mourad:
New Moroccan,
by Mourad
Lahlou.

Maybe you think tea is something only adults love. But after I tried Moroccan mint tea, I couldn't get enough of the stuff. In most restaurants we visited, we were served a hot pot of mint tea. I'm not just talking about some water with mint in it. It starts with gunpowder green tea, which tastes kinda savory. That's balanced out by a boatload of mint (who doesn't love mint?), sugar, and, if you want, a little citrusy kick of lemon verbena. This tea is sweet, warming, and refreshing all at the same time; it reminds me of the chai my mom always made when I was growing up. This recipe comes from Mourad Lahlou, a Moroccan American chef in San Francisco who will make a tea lover out of you.

1 tablespoon loose gunpowder green tea (2 tea bags work, too!)

¼ cup sugar

1 large bunch mint

1 lemon verbena sprig (optional)

1 Bring 4 cups water to a boil in a small pot over high heat. Once the water is boiling rapidly (you'll see lots of big bubbles), turn the heat down to medium and add the tea. Let the tea simmer for 5 minutes. Add the sugar, mint, and lemon verbena, if using. Stir to dissolve the sugar and use a spoon to push the sprigs down so they are completely submerged. Turn the heat up to medium-high, and let simmer for another 3 minutes. Remove the pot from the heat, cover with a lid, and let the tea steep for 3 minutes.

2 Using a tea strainer or any other kind of mesh strainer, strain the tea into a teapot to serve.

Morocco

ENGLAND

Feeling fancy with my tower of teeny sandwiches and scones at high tea.

Outside Buckingham Palace. It's hard to believe some countries still have kings and queens!

There are so many cool buildings in London, like this giant clock tower called Big Ben!

I could take a million trips to England. I like London the best, probably because that's where I've spent the most of my time; I even lived there during college! I love it all: the postcard-gorgeous cobblestone streets, the teatime rituals, all the cool sights to see (Victoria Gardens! London Bridge!), and even the cloudy weather.

The Brits love teatime and especially tea snacks—wee sandwiches and crumbly pastries that make you feel so fancy—and stick-to-your-ribs hearty fare, like a classic English breakfast with beans, toast, sausage, and eggs. And of course there's the Indian food. The British violently colonized India for hundreds of years, and the relationship between those two countries is complicated. But because so many Indians now live in England, the quality of the Indian food there is fantastic. In fact, the food in England gets better and better every time I visit, and it's largely thanks to all the people from different cultures who call the country home.

Here are some of my favorite cookbooks by British authors:

Cook As You Are by Ruby Tandoh

Nadiya's British Food Adventure by Nadiya Hussain

DAD'S ENGLISH BREAKFAST

Serves

4

" Tasted great, easy to make.

—MADELINE, 5

I love a hotel breakfast. (Buffet? Yes, please!) Especially when that hotel breakfast is in England. One time we stayed at a tiny inn where a hearty English breakfast was served—toast, eggs, baked beans, tomatoes, and onions and potatoes that were cooked till they were charred and roasty. Back home in Dallas, my parents make their own English breakfast. This recipe, courtesy of my dad, is simple, but if you want to do as my dad does, doctor it up with your favorite spice blend. He loves chaat masala. My niece Madeline loves everything bagel seasoning. Anything punchy will work.

* HOT TIP FROM MY DAD

"You can warm up a can of baked beans as an accompaniment to the toast and double the enjoyment!"

1 medium yellow potato

2 Roma tomatoes

1 medium red onion

2 tablespoons olive oil

Toasted bread with butter, for serving

Kosher salt and freshly ground black pepper, for serving

1 Poke the potato 5 times on each side with a fork. Microwave the potato in a microwave-safe bowl for 6 minutes, flipping it halfway through. It should be soft but not mushy, maintaining some firmness. Once the potato is cool enough to handle, cut it into 4 even slices.

2 Slice the tomatoes in half crosswise. Cut the ends off each side.

3 Slice the onion into 4 even slices. Make sure to keep the rings together in each slice.

4 Warm the olive oil in a large nonstick skillet over high heat for a minute. Arrange all the slices of potato and onion and the tomato halves in the skillet, avoiding overlap. Let them cook over high heat until the bottoms are browned, 3 to 5 minutes. Flip and let the other side cook until browned, another 3 to 5 minutes. Turn the heat down to medium, cover with a lid, and cook until the onions have softened and you can slice into them like butter, about 4 minutes.

5 Serve everything with the buttered toast and let each diner season with salt and pepper to taste.

MY DAD'S SERVING SUGGESTION

⊐→ Arrange a slice each of potato and onion and a tomato half on a slice of toasted, buttered crusty bread. Top with more salt and black pepper, if desired.

167

TEA SANDWICHES

Makes
As many sandwiches as you'd like!

Very simple and yummy. I liked the crispy cucumbers.

—ETHAN, 9

Teatime will always be one of my favorite parts about visiting London. Even if you don't like tea, the snacks and sweets served alongside it will make the experience great. And no teatime is complete without teeny-tiny crustless sandwiches that you can pop in your mouth, two or three at a time. The two kinds I especially love are cucumber sandwiches and smoked salmon sandwiches. Cucumber sandwiches have this clean, refreshing flavor. Smoked salmon, on the other hand, is so salty and delicious. These recipes come from my brother-in-law, David, who lives in England. His advice? Make sure your bread is soft. "This is not time for chewy sourdough or a crusty whole wheat loaf!" he says.

TRADITIONAL CUCUMBER TEA SANDWICHES

1 English cucumber, peeled and sliced into thin rounds

Kosher salt

White bread

Unsalted butter, at room temperature (it should be softened but not melty)

Freshly ground black pepper

Place the cucumber rounds in a colander. Lightly salt them and let sit for 15 to 20 minutes. Afterward, lay out some paper towels, place the cucumber slices on top, and pat them dry.

Build your sandwiches. Lay out slices of white bread and cut off the crusts. Slather each slice with butter. Layer half the slices of bread with the cucumber rounds, overlapping each round slightly. Sprinkle with pepper. Top with the remaining slices of bread. Cut in half to make rectangular sandwiches. Serve immediately.

CUCUMBER TEA SANDWICHES WITH CREAM CHEESE

 1 English cucumber, peeled and sliced into thin rounds

Kosher salt

8 ounces whipped cream cheese

½ cup chopped fresh dill

White bread

Freshly ground black pepper

Place the cucumber rounds in a colander. Lightly salt them and let sit for 15 to 20 minutes. Afterward, lay out some paper towels, place the cucumber slices on top, and pat them dry.

Mix the cream cheese and dill together in a small bowl. Season with salt to taste.

Build your sandwiches. Lay out slices of white bread and cut off the crusts. Slather each slice with the cream cheese mixture. Layer half the slices of bread with the cucumber rounds, overlapping each round slightly. Sprinkle with pepper. Top with the remaining slices of bread. Cut in half to make rectangular sandwiches. Serve immediately.

SMOKED SALMON TEA SANDWICHES WITH HERB BUTTER

½ cup (1 stick) unsalted butter, at room temperature (it should be softened but not melty)

 1 tablespoon chopped fresh dill

1 tablespoon chopped fresh chives

1 tablespoon chopped fresh parsley

1 teaspoon freshly squeezed lemon juice

Kosher salt

Brown bread, like pumpernickel

8 ounces smoked salmon

Mix the butter, dill, chives, parsley, and lemon juice together in a small bowl. Season with salt to taste.

Build your sandwiches. Lay out slices of brown bread and cut off the crusts. Slather each slice with the herb butter. Layer half the slices of bread with smoked salmon. Top with the remaining slices of bread and cut in half to make rectangular sandwiches. Serve immediately.

England

SCONES

Makes

8

scones

" The recipe was
really delicious!
The scones were
light and fluffy,
and they paired
perfectly with
the strawberry
jam and clotted
cream.

—RADHIKA, 11

When I was in middle school, my sister, Meera, went to London . . . without
me. In fairness, she went for a school trip. But when she came back, she
had a camera full of memories that I could not wait to comb through. In
one photo, she and her friends were dressed nicely, drinking little cups
of tea, and eating from a tower of snacks that included teensy cucumber
sandwiches (pages 146 and 147) and . . . scones! Just from the picture of the
crumbly, buttery pastries smeared with jam and clotted cream (which is like
sour cream but softer and richer!), I knew that I would love scones. So when
my mom and I went to London together a few years later, we made a beeline
to what the British call "high tea" for the scones. They were even better than
what I had imagined from the photo.

¾ cup (1½ sticks) unsalted
butter, very cold

3 cups (420 grams) all-
purpose flour, plus more for
dusting

½ cup (100 grams)
granulated sugar

1½ teaspoons baking
powder

½ teaspoon baking soda

 Zest of ½ lemon (get an adult
to help you use a zester!)

1 teaspoon kosher salt

½ cup (75 grams) currants or
raisins (optional)

1 cup (240 grams)
buttermilk, very cold

Cooking spray, for greasing

1 tablespoon unsalted
butter, melted then cooled
slightly, for brushing

2 tablespoons coarse
sugar (such as Demerara,
turbinado, or similar), for
topping

Toppings of your choice:
strawberry jam, clotted
cream, butter, bacon,
Nutella, whatever you'd like!

1 Cut the 1½ sticks of very cold butter into pecan-size pieces and return it to the refrigerator while you mix your dry ingredients.

2 Mix the flour, granulated sugar, baking powder, baking soda, lemon zest, and salt together in a large bowl just until combined. Have two butter knives ready. Add the pieces of very cold butter to the bowl and, working quickly, slice the knives across each other in the bowl as if you were cutting up pancakes into little pieces (you can also use your fingers and squish the butter!). Work from one edge of the bowl across to the other, then turn your bowl a quarter turn and repeat the cutting motion. The goal here is to cut the butter into small pieces within the flour mixture while it is still very cold. Continue this cutting motion until the butter is in small pea-size pieces, with a few larger pecan-size pieces here and there (these larger bits will help make the scones nice and flaky).

3 Next, add the currants or raisins (if using) to the flour mix and quickly toss with a spoon to combine.

4 Pour the buttermilk into the flour mixture and mix lightly with a spatula or spoon just until it is mixed in. At this point it will look like a shaggy mess, but don't worry. Using your hands, gently pat and squeeze the dough just until it starts to come together and feels like Play-Doh. Try your best to do this part quickly; too much handling and the butter will start to melt.

Dump the dough out onto a kitchen counter coated generously with more flour and loosely pat it (or roll with a rolling pin) into a rectangle about 1 inch thick.

 Next, take a glass about 3 inches in diameter and spray the rim with a bit of cooking spray (alternatively, you can dip it in a bit of flour). Press the rim of the glass into the dough, rotating it back and forth to prevent it from sticking. Gently remove the dough circle from the glass and set it aside. Repeat until you have cut out 8 circles. You can also use your favorite cookie cutter or make your own shapes! You might have a bit of extra dough; you can reroll it and cut out another circle or two, but try not to do this more than once or your scones will start to get tough.

 Line a sheet pan with parchment paper and place the dough circles on it, spaced at least 2 inches apart. Using your fingers or a pastry brush, brush the tops of the scones lightly with the melted butter and sprinkle with the coarse sugar. Let the scones rest in the fridge for about 15 minutes.

 While the scones are in the fridge, preheat the oven to 425°F, with a rack in the middle of the oven. Bake the scones for 10 minutes. Lower the oven temperature to 350°F (no need to wait for the temperature to reduce) and continue to bake for 15 to 20 minutes more, until lightly golden brown.

 Serve the scones warm with strawberry jam and clotted cream (my favorite), or any of the other toppings. The scones taste best the day they are made but can be frozen and reheated in a 300°F oven for about 10 minutes.

England

INDIA

Fishing for our
dinner in Kerala!

The Taj Mahal probably the coolest
building I've ever seen.

I love the sari shops in India. So many colors!

My parents are originally from India, so when I was growing up, we would make regular trips there to see family. India is one of the most fascinating countries you can visit— every city is different, the energy is electric, and being there feels like stepping into a different world, with all the colors and sounds and the street food (*wowwwwie*, the street food is delicious). We didn't always feel like tourists, as we were often with cousins and we could speak one of the local languages, Hindi! This chapter contains just a few of the dishes that make me think of India. Of course, I grew up eating Indian food at home, but going to India was so cool because even as someone who was regularly eating Indian food, I realized that each part of India has its own cuisine, and all of them are amazing.

If you want to learn more about the cuisine of India, check out these cookbooks:

Indian-ish by me, Priya Krishna! (Shameless plug, but I love my own cookbook, and I think you will, too!)

Made in India by Meera Sodha

At Home with Madhur Jaffrey by Madhur Jaffrey

PALAKKAD SHRIMP CURRY

Serves
4 to 6

I may never again eat as well as I did on my family trip to Kerala. My family hails from Uttar Pradesh, in the North; so when we visited Kerala, which is in the South, I tasted a completely different set of flavors. One night, a chef in our hotel restaurant did a cooking demonstration where he made this shrimp dish. I was absolutely mesmerized. The tangy tamarind, the creamy coconut milk, the aroma of the spices—and all of it cooked with plump pieces of shrimp. I dreamed about this dish night after night. So you can imagine my excitement when my mom told me that her friend Shanti Dev, who spent several summers at his grandmother's place in Palakkad, Kerala, had a recipe for this exact shrimp dish. There are a lot of steps, but you can do it! The yummy, complex flavor is worth it.

"Loved everything about it! The texture, the taste. Everything!"
—MAYA, 8

For the shrimp marinade

1 pound (20 to 30) fresh shrimp (buy them deveined and with the shell removed; the tails can be on or off)

1 garlic clove, crushed (the bottom of a can works well for this)

 1 teaspoon minced fresh ginger

1 teaspoon red chile powder (such as cayenne or Kashmiri)

½ teaspoon ground turmeric

½ teaspoon kosher salt

½ teaspoon freshly ground black pepper

1 tablespoon freshly squeezed lemon juice

For the sauce

2 tablespoons olive oil or coconut oil

½ teaspoon black mustard seeds

½ teaspoon fenugreek seeds

½ teaspoon cumin seeds

10 to 12 fresh curry leaves (these can be purchased at any Indian grocery store)

1½ teaspoons minced fresh ginger

1 garlic clove, crushed

1 medium yellow onion, diced

1 medium tomato, diced

1 teaspoon ground coriander

1 teaspoon red chile powder (such as cayenne or Kashmiri)

½ teaspoon ground turmeric

1 (13.5-ounce) can coconut milk

1 tablespoon tamarind paste or concentrate

Kosher salt, if needed

¼ cup chopped fresh cilantro (stems and leaves), for garnish

Cooked rice or roti, for serving

India

1 **Marinate the shrimp.** Pat the shrimp dry with a paper towel. Wash your hands afterward! Mix the garlic, ginger, chile powder, turmeric, salt, and pepper in a large bowl. Add the shrimp and lemon juice and gently rub the marinade into the shrimp with your hands. Wash your hands again! Cover the bowl and let the shrimp rest in the fridge for 2 hours. Set it on the counter 30 minutes before you start cooking.

2   **Make the sauce.** Lay the rest of the ingredients out next to the stove, for easy access. Warm the oil in a large deep pan or Dutch oven over medium heat. When the oil is hot, add the mustard seeds. Once you hear the mustard seeds make popping sounds, 1 to 3 minutes, turn the heat down to low and add the fenugreek seeds, cumin seeds, and curry leaves. When you add the curry leaves, they will sputter—be careful! This part moves fast and there might be mild splattering! Ask an adult to help.

3 Once the curry leaves are done dancing, add the ginger, garlic, and onions and turn the heat up to medium. Cook until the onions become soft and wilted, 5 to 10 minutes, stirring every so often so they don't brown.

4   Add the tomato, coriander, chile powder, and turmeric and cook and stir until you can smell the aroma of the mixed spices, about 2 minutes.

5   Mix the coconut milk and tamarind paste into the curry, then mix in ½ cup water, cover the pan with a lid, and let the curry cook until it has become a thick sauce, like a gravy, 5 to 7 minutes.

6   Add the marinated shrimp to the pan and cook, uncovered, until the shrimp turn pink all over, 3 to 4 minutes. Taste and see if the dish needs salt. If it does, add a little more.

7   Transfer to a serving dish and garnish with the cilantro. Serve with rice or roti.

Serves
4

DAHI BHALLA, NANA STYLE

The street vendors of India are probably some of the greatest cooks in the world. They make dishes that mix sweet with salty, creamy with crunchy, spicy with sour. They know how to achieve that perfect balance. My favorite bites when I visit are always enjoyed not in a restaurant but at a roadside stand. This is my ode to one of my favorite vendors, a guy who exclusively makes dahi bhalla—essentially fritters soaked in yogurt and topped with all kinds of chutneys. Frying at home can be annoying, so my nana, or grandfather, developed this quick version, which substitutes microwaved potato slices for the fritters. They do just as good a job of soaking up the creamy yogurt and all of the chutneys.

1 teaspoon ground cumin

1 teaspoon kosher salt

1½ cups plain full-fat yogurt (not Greek)

4 medium yellow potatoes

1 (15-ounce) can chickpeas, drained and rinsed (optional)

½ cup store-bought tamarind chutney

½ teaspoon red chile powder (such as cayenne or Kashmiri)

 ¼ cup chopped fresh cilantro leaves, for garnish

¼ cup sev (a crispy chickpea topping available in most Indian grocery stores; optional)

1 Toast the cumin in a small pan over low heat until it turns a shade darker and you can really smell it, 7 to 10 minutes. Set aside.

2 Combine ½ teaspoon of the salt and the yogurt in a small bowl and whisk until smooth.

3 Poke the potatoes 5 times on each side with a fork and microwave them, uncovered, in a large microwave-safe plate or bowl for 10 minutes, flipping them halfway through. Once the potatoes are cool enough to handle, slice them into disks (about ½ inch thick should work).

4 Arrange the potato slices in an even layer with a little overlap on a medium serving platter. Sprinkle the remaining ½ teaspoon salt over the potatoes. Pour the salted yogurt over the top, followed by the chickpeas, if using, then the tamarind chutney. Sprinkle with the chile powder and the toasted cumin. Garnish with the chopped cilantro and the sev, if using.

Arrange the potato
slices on a platter and
sprinkle with salt.

Pour the yogurt over
the potatoes.

Add some chickpeas
if you'd like.

Drizzle with the chutney.

Sprinkle with the spices.

Garnish with cilantro
and sev, if using.

SHAHI TOAST

Serves

4

This was one of my mom's favorite desserts as a kid growing up in India. Think of shahi toast as the ultimate bread pudding—creamy, dreamy, and infused with cardamom, which tastes citrusy, sweet, and floral. This is my mom's shortcut version; this recipe originally appeared in my cookbook *Indian-ish*, and I'm sharing it here with some upgrades (hint: butter). It is amazing how luxurious this tastes, considering how easy it is to make—my favorite kind of dessert!

2 cups heavy cream

6 tablespoons sugar

1 teaspoon ground cardamom

½ teaspoon kosher salt

2 tablespoons unsalted butter

5 slices white bread, crusts removed, each slice cut into 4 squares

2 tablespoons roughly chopped pistachios, for garnish

1 Coat the bottom of a medium pot or a small Dutch oven with 2 tablespoons water (this will prevent the cream from sticking when you heat it up), and then add the cream. Cook over medium heat, stirring regularly, until the cream is warmed through, 4 to 6 minutes. Turn off the heat and stir in the sugar, cardamom, and salt, making sure the sugar dissolves completely. Set aside.

Melt the butter in a large skillet over medium-high heat. Once the butter is melted, turn the heat down to medium-low, add the bread, and cook until the bottom is golden brown, 4 to 6 minutes. Flip carefully using tongs and cook until the other side is also golden brown, 4 to 6 minutes more.

 Arrange the pieces of bread in a single layer, like a patchwork quilt, in a 9-inch square baking dish. Give the cardamom cream a stir to fully incorporate the sugar and cardamom, then pour it over the bread, making sure each piece of bread is fully soaked with the cream mixture.

 Cover the dish with plastic wrap and refrigerate overnight or for up to 12 hours. Just before serving, garnish with the pistachios.

SALTY OR SWEET LASSI

Whenever we stayed with my aunt and uncle in Delhi in the summer when I was growing up, they would make us salty lassi in the morning. In the sweltering Indian heat, there is nothing more refreshing than cold, creamy yogurt spiked with herbs, with a little kick of pepper. If salty beverages aren't your thing, try making sweet lassi, which you can add mango to for a tangier, more colorful drink. And when you blend the lassi, my tip is to not totally blend the ice but instead leave a few little ice granules, which make the drink even more thirst quenching.

SALTY LASSI

2 cups plain full-fat yogurt (not Greek)

¼ teaspoon kosher salt

½ teaspoon freshly ground black pepper

2 cilantro sprigs

7 fresh mint leaves

2 large ice cubes, plus more for serving

Combine the yogurt, salt, pepper, cilantro, 5 of the mint leaves, and the ice cubes in a blender and blend on high speed until everything is well incorporated and the ice has become tiny granules.

Pour into four glasses filled with a few more ice cubes. Tear the remaining 2 mint leaves into pieces and use as a garnish. Serve immediately.

SWEET LASSI

2 cups plain full-fat yogurt (not Greek)

½ cup sugar

2 large ice cubes, plus more for serving

1 cup mango pulp (optional, if you want to make it a mango lassi)

 Combine the yogurt, sugar, ice cubes, and mango pulp (if using) in a blender and blend on high speed until everything is well incorporated and the ice has become tiny granules.

Pour into four glasses filled with a few more ice cubes. Serve immediately.

TOKYO SUBWAY
24-hour ticket 600円

KIT KAT

JAPAN

I could have spent the whole trip at all the Japanese markets that sell stationery and toys!

In front of the Great Buddha of Kamakura. The biggest Buddha I'd ever seen!

When I imagine what the cities of the future will look like, I picture Tokyo. Because from the minute we landed, that's what it felt like. It was as if we had walked into the year 2070. We ordered miso ramen from a vending machine, and the trains seemed to travel at the speed of a bullet (that's why they're called bullet trains). And Japan is so much more than Tokyo. We were lucky enough to travel up into the mountains to stay in a ryokan, an incredibly peaceful inn. And best of all, we traveled by train, which not only is super fast but meant we got to eat bento boxes! Bento boxes are like a lunch box meets treasure chest, with different kinds of foods in each compartment (you can learn how to make your own on page 174).

One last funny story: my dad has this safari vest where he keeps all our passports and money when we travel (you know how dads are). But when we got to Tokyo and were riding the bus to the hotel, my dad took off his vest and put it in a compartment on the bus . . . and left it there. He was so stressed out! How were we going to get back to the US without our passports? But then, within a half hour, the hotel had tracked down the bus, located my dad's vest, and returned it to us, nicely folded up! If that's not the most well-run city I've ever visited, I don't know what is.

If you want to learn more about the cuisine of Japan, check out these cookbooks:

Japanese Home Cooking by Sonoko Sakai
Just One Cookbook by Namiko Chen
Japanese Cookbook for Beginners by Azusa Oda

HOW TO BENTO!

Bento boxes are a standard meal format in Japan, a way of creating a balanced meal of pre-portioned foods, usually some kind of meat, rice or noodles, and vegetables. And in every train station I visited in Japan, I could always find an assortment of bentos, each one filled with different foods, like tonkatsu (fried pork) or tamagoyaki (rolled omelet). Such a fun way to eat. This guide to making your own bento is courtesy of the amazing Namiko Chen, who runs the blog *Just One Cookbook*. Namiko has also given us a recipe for one of her favorite bentos to make for her family—chicken meatballs (page 175)! You can pair the meatballs with some sliced cucumbers and rice, or whatever you want! And if chicken meatballs aren't your thing, take a look at her guide below and design your own bento.

NAMIKO SAYS . . .

① **Get a bento box.** It doesn't have to be a Japanese one. It can be any kind of container with a lid (even better if it has multiple compartments).

② **Get silicone cups (optional).** If my container does not have multiple compartments, I like to use silicone cups (or cupcake cups), which will help keep dry food separate from wet food, and will hold loose items like blueberries in place.

③ **Get sauce containers.** If you want to pack a sauce, like soy sauce or peanut sauce, you can buy portable sauce containers. Any tiny bottle or jar will do.

④ **Plan your bento box!** I try to organize my bento like the following:

▷▸ **Cooked rice or noodles:** I like short-grain rice or soba or udon noodles

▷▸ **Main:** Meat, fish, or other seafood

▷▸ **Sides:** Steamed or stir-fried vegetables, rolled omelet, potato salad

▷▸ **Fillers:** Simple yet colorful ingredients (cherry tomatoes, carrots, boiled egg sliced in half) to brighten the bento

▷▸ **Fruits:** Berries, grapes, apples (in the bento box or in a separate container)

TIPS FOR A GREAT BENTO

An assortment of colors in your food is always nice! It's pretty to look at, and it means you're eating a variety of fruits and vegetables.

Make extra portions! If you are making the chicken meatballs recipe in this book (opposite), try doubling it and putting the rest in the freezer. That way, the next time you are making a bento, you won't have to start from scratch.

The order in which you pack your bento box matters! Start with the bulkiest dish, like rice, then add your protein, and then use the side dishes to fill in the gaps.

Pack your food tightly! Otherwise, when you open your bento, everything will be messy!

CHICKEN MEATBALLS

Serves
4

This is one of Namiko's favorite foods to put in her kids' bento boxes. These meatballs pack a yummy punch and are fun to roll. You can pair them with just about anything—noodles, rice, broccoli, cucumbers, carrots. Make sure the meatballs are well coated in the sauce; that's what gives them so much flavor.

> " *Little hands like making gooey meatballs.*
>
> —MILO, 6

For the sauce

1 tablespoon soy sauce

1 tablespoon sugar

1 tablespoon mirin

2 teaspoons rice wine vinegar

½ teaspoon potato starch or cornstarch

For the meatballs

5 ounces firm tofu (about a third of a 14-ounce block)

14 ounces ground chicken

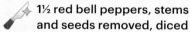 1½ red bell peppers, stems and seeds removed, diced

1 scallion, sliced

1 large egg

1 teaspoon minced fresh ginger

1 teaspoon kosher salt

A few cracks freshly ground black pepper

Vegetable or canola oil, for cooking

 1 **Make the sauce.** Whisk together the soy sauce, sugar, mirin, vinegar, and potato starch in a small bowl and set aside.

 2 **Make the meatballs.** Wrap the tofu with a clean towel and let it drain for 15 minutes—the water should soak the towel.

recipe continues →

Japan

Place the ground chicken in a large bowl and add the bell peppers and scallion. Break up the drained tofu by hand into small pieces and mix into the chicken. Add the egg, ginger, salt, and black pepper. Mix again. Using two tablespoons or a cookie scoop, make small meatballs and set them on a plate or a sheet of foil or parchment paper. Wash your hands afterward.

  Pour a thin layer of oil into a large nonstick skillet over medium heat. Once the oil is hot, carefully add the meatballs, keeping some distance between them. All the meatballs might not fit into the pan at once, and that's okay. You can always cook a second batch. Be careful about oil splattering; don't get too close to the pan!

Cook until the bottoms of the meatballs are nicely browned (use a spatula to peek under one), 5 to 7 minutes, then flip them over, cover with a lid, and keep cooking until the inside is no longer pink, about 3 more minutes. You can cut into one with a fork or knife to check this. If the meatballs start to burn on the bottom, reduce the heat to medium-low.

 If you have more meatballs to cook, do that now. Just remove the first batch of meatballs from the pan and add a little extra oil. Once you're done, add the first round of meatballs back to the pan.

 Pour the sauce you made earlier into the pan; it should start to bubble and thicken. Turn the meatballs to coat all sides with the sauce, and you're done!

 To store, transfer the leftovers to an airtight container with the sauce, let cool completely, and keep in the refrigerator for up to 3 days or in the freezer for a month.

LIFE-CHANGING UDON

WITH SOFT-BOILED EGG, HOT SOY SAUCE, AND BLACK PEPPER

Difficulty Level: EASY

Serves
4

"We all enjoyed it!
—MILO, 6

Recipe from
To Asia, With Love
by Hetty McKinnon.

In the debate over rice or noodles, I choose noodles. Dishes like this remind me why. Noodles come in so many shapes and sizes and textures. The type of noodle can make one dish feel entirely different from another one. A big favorite is udon, a thick, extra-chewy noodle. The first time I had udon was in Japan, and it was in a noodle soup that was perfectly rich and salty. My friend the cookbook author Hetty McKinnon had a similar experience in Tokyo, and this is her ode to that life-changing udon. No exaggeration: this is one of my favorite noodle dishes I have ever cooked.

4 large eggs

1 (28-ounce) package fresh, vacuum-sealed, or frozen udon noodles or 16 ounces dried

2 cups vegetable broth

¼ cup tamari or soy sauce

2 teaspoons mirin

6 tablespoons salted butter, cut into 4 cubes

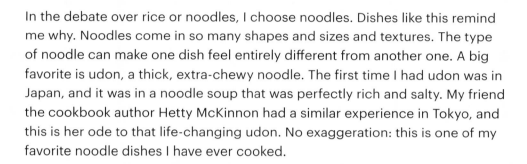 4 scallions, sliced

Freshly ground black pepper, for garnish

Toasted sesame oil, for garnish

Japan

177

1   Bring a small pot of water to a boil over high heat. Carefully add the eggs and set a timer for 6 minutes. As soon as the timer is up, immediately—and again, carefully—scoop the eggs out of the water with a slotted spoon and place under cold running water until they are completely cold. (This will make very soft-boiled eggs—if you prefer a firmer yolk, cook the eggs for another minute.) Peel and set aside.

2   Bring a large pot of water seasoned with a large pinch of salt to a boil over high heat. Add the udon and cook according to the package instructions. This will take 1 to 3 minutes for fresh, vacuum sealed, or frozen udon, or a few more minutes for dried udon. Drain, then scoop the hot noodles into four bowls.

3   While the water for the udon is coming to a boil, combine the broth, tamari, and mirin in the small pot you used to boil the eggs and place over low heat until hot.

4   Divide the hot broth among the bowls of noodles and top each with a soft-boiled egg cut in half lengthwise. Add a cube of butter to each bowl and allow it to melt into the noodles. Add the scallions and a generous amount of pepper (use as much pepper as you'd like, but this dish is intended to be very peppery). Finish each bowl with a little drizzle of sesame oil.

Japan

Serves

4

ZARU SOBA

Soba is one of my favorite types of noodles—they're so chewy, and they have such a distinct flavor that you can slurp them by themselves! In Japan, there were so many shops devoted just to making soba. They made the noodles fresh and served them on a bamboo mat, with a flavorful dipping sauce. With this simple recipe, which comes from my friend Namiko, I like to make double the noodle soup base and keep it around in my fridge, so whenever the soba craving hits, all I have to do is boil noodles.

For the mentsuyu (dipping sauce)

¼ cup sake

½ cup soy sauce

½ cup mirin

1 (1-inch-square) piece kombu (dried kelp)

1 cup katsuobushi (dried bonito flakes; they are fluffy, so pack them down when you measure)

14 ounces dried soba noodles

For the toppings

1 sheet nori (dried seaweed)

2 scallions, sliced

✳ NOTE

Sake is an alcoholic drink for adults, but when it's heated, the alcohol gets cooked off. You can also buy cooking sake, which has a lower alcohol content, at any Asian grocery store.

1 **Make the dipping sauce.** Bring the sake to a boil in a medium saucepan over medium-high heat. Once it's bubbling, let it boil for a few seconds and then add the soy sauce, mirin, kombu, and katsuobushi. Wait for the mixture to come back to a boil and then turn the heat down to low and cook for 5 minutes. Remove from the heat and let cool completely.

2 Strain the sauce through a sieve or colander into a bowl so that all you have is the liquid. Discard the kombu and katsuobushi. You can keep the sauce in an airtight container in the refrigerator for up to a month.

3 **Make the noodles.** Fill a large pot a little over halfway with water and bring to a boil over high heat. Add the soba and cook according to the package instructions, stirring the noodles once in a while so they don't stick to one another. When they're cooked, they should be soft but still chewy. Carefully drain the noodles and rinse them under cold water.

4 To serve, divide the noodles among four plates. Crumble the nori on top of the noodles and shower them with the scallions. Set out four bowls and put 6 tablespoons of dipping sauce in each. Add 1¼ cups ice-cold water to each of the four bowls with the sauce. Check the taste. If it is too salty, add more water.

5 Let everyone dip the noodles in sauce as they please.

If you want to mix things up, try the soba coated in peanut sauce!

SOBA WITH PEANUT SAUCE

For the peanut sauce

½ cup peanut butter

¼ cup warm water

 3 garlic cloves, minced

3 tablespoons soy sauce

3 tablespoons rice wine vinegar

1 tablespoon sriracha, or other chili sauce

1 tablespoon sugar

1½ teaspoons minced fresh ginger

2 teaspoons toasted sesame oil

Mix the sauce ingredients together in a small bowl. In a large bowl, toss the noodles and vegetables with the sauce.

For the assembly

Large handful of vegetables (such as cucumbers, cabbage, and carrots), sliced into thin pieces

Sliced scallions, for garnish

Sesame seeds, for garnish

Garnish with scallions and sesame seeds.

MISO RAMEN

Serves
4

" I loved the
spiciness.
It tasted
AMAZING. I like
how the hotness
lingered in my
mouth!

—FINN, 7½

Before I visited Japan, the only ramen I ever ate came out of packets. Don't get me wrong: those are delicious. But my trip unlocked a whole new level of ramen—painstakingly made broths that took hours and hours to cook and hand-rolled noodles with a perfect springiness. The first time my dad ordered ramen in Japan, he immediately asked for chili sauce, and the chef shook his head, as he had spent hours making a brilliantly balanced broth (though I promise this recipe doesn't take forever).

I haven't even gotten to the incredible ramen vending machines—basically, you go to a shop, select what you want via a button, get a ticket, and boom! Ramen appears at the counter just a few minutes later. My favorite bowls of ramen were ones with a miso broth. Miso, a paste made by fermenting soybeans, makes ramen taste rich and savory. This version, which comes from my friend Namiko, is an ode to all the miso ramen I loved in Japan.

For the broth

1 tablespoon toasted sesame oil

2 garlic cloves, crushed (the bottom of a can works well for this)

½ teaspoon minced fresh ginger

1 shallot, minced

4 ounces ground pork

1 teaspoon doubanjiang (spicy chili bean sauce/broad bean paste, available from Asian grocery stores)

3 tablespoons white miso

1 tablespoon toasted white sesame seeds, coarsely ground (use a mortar and pestle or put the seeds in a resealable bag and roll over them with a rolling pin; ask an adult to help with this!)

1 tablespoon sugar

1 tablespoon sake (see the note on page 180)

4 cups chicken broth

¼ teaspoon ground white pepper

Kosher salt (optional)

10 to 12 ounces fresh ramen noodles or 6 to 8 ounces dried

Optional toppings

Bean sprouts, microwaved for 2 minutes

Baby bok choy, trimmed and microwaved for 2 minutes

Frozen or canned corn

Nori sheets (dried seaweed), crumbled

Sliced scallions

1 🔥 **Make the broth.** In a medium pot, warm the sesame oil over medium-low heat. Add the garlic, ginger, and shallot. With a wooden spatula or spoon, stir-fry until the smell fills your kitchen.

2 Add the pork and increase the heat to medium. Cook until the pork is no longer pink, a few minutes, using the wooden spatula to break it up as it cooks.

3 Add the doubanjiang and miso and quickly mix them in with the meat. Add the ground sesame seeds and sugar and mix well. Add the sake and chicken broth and turn the heat up to high, bringing the soup to a boil (it will bubble a lot!), then turn the heat down to medium. Add the white pepper, then taste your soup for salt, adding some if necessary. (Each brand of chicken broth varies in saltiness, so you will have to taste your soup to decide how much salt to add.) Cover the pot with a lid and keep the soup simmering while you cook the noodles.

4 To cook the ramen noodles, bring a large pot of water to a boil. Cook the noodles according to the package instructions. I usually cook them about 15 seconds less than the suggested cooking time. When the noodles are done, drain them using a sieve or colander and divide them among four bowls.

5 Add ramen broth to each bowl. Place the toppings of your choice on top of the noodles and serve immediately.

SALMON ONIGIRI

In Japan, I was mesmerized by the food at the konbini, aka convenience stores. Here I found all manner of Japanese candy—matcha Kit Kats! sakura gummies!—yummy fruit sandwiches, mochi, and best of all: onigiri! Onigiri is a portable snack made with rice—the fillings range from pickled plum to chicken to my personal favorite, salmon! The filling is hidden in the rice like a surprise, and it all comes dressed in a seaweed jacket. This recipe is from my friend Namiko, who often makes onigiri with her family. Her tip: make sure to wet your hands when you are shaping the onigiri because the rice is sticky.

Serves

4

" I liked the
texture.
—FINN, 7½

For the steamed rice

2 cups uncooked
Japanese short-grain rice

For the filling

Kosher salt

1 salmon fillet

For making the onigiri

4 sheets nori (dried
seaweed)

Kosher salt

Toasted white and
black sesame seeds, for
garnish

1 **Make the rice.** Put the rice in a large bowl, add enough tap water to cover the rice, and wash it, using your hands to swish the grains around. Discard the water. Repeat this process 3 or 4 times. Let the rice soak in water for 30 minutes. Transfer the rice to a sieve and drain completely, for at least 15 minutes.

2 Combine the rice and 2½ cups water in a medium deep pot. Cover the pot with a lid and bring to a boil over medium heat. Once the water is boiling, turn the heat down to low and continue to cook, covered, until the water is completely absorbed, 12 to 13 minutes. At the 12- to 13-minute mark, take a quick peek, and if you see any water left, cover and continue cooking for another minute or so.

recipe continues →

Japan

187

3   Remove the pot from the heat and let it sit, covered, for another 10 minutes. Let the cooked rice cool a little bit, until you can hold the rice without burning your hands (it helps to spread it out on a sheet pan). But do *not* let the rice cool down completely.

4   **Make the filling.** While the rice is cooking and cooling, prepare the onigiri filling. Preheat the oven to 425°F. Sprinkle a little salt on both sides of the salmon fillet, and place the fillet on a small sheet pan or baking dish. Bake for 10 to 20 minutes, until the salmon flakes easily when you poke at it with a fork.

5   Break the cooked salmon into flakes and set it aside, discarding the skin (or you can eat it; I think it's tasty!).

6   **Assemble the onigiri.** While the rice is cooling, cut the nori into 1½-inch-wide strips.

7   Wet your hands in order to prevent the rice from sticking to them. Put some salt on your hands—I like to dip three fingertips in kosher salt—and rub to spread it all around your palms.

8   Scoop out a handful (about ⅓ cup) of warm rice into one hand. Create a small indentation in the center of the rice. Put 1 to 2 teaspoons of salmon inside. Then mold the rice with your hands around the indentation to cover the filling completely.

9   Gently form the rice into a triangle. I use three fingers (thumb, pointer finger, middle finger) to make a triangle corner. Your hands should be just firm enough so the onigiri doesn't fall apart. You don't want to squeeze the rice too tightly.

10 Wrap the nori around the onigiri, like you're wrapping a blanket around a baby, then sprinkle the top point that's not wrapped in nori with sesame seeds. You can also wrap the seaweed over the bottom of the onigiri, like a flap or a diaper, and sprinkle sesame seeds along the other two sides. If your hands get too messy, wipe them off and re-dip them in water and salt before you make the next one. Repeat these steps with all the rice.

11 Eat the onigiri immediately, as the rice gets hard when you refrigerate it. But if you really need to wait to eat them, there's a trick: wrap the whole tray of onigiri with thick kitchen towels and store in the fridge. Bring to room temperature before eating.

The perfect after-school snack!

Wet your hands and spread salt on your palms.

Scoop rice into one hand and make an indentation in the middle.

Put salmon in the indentation.

Mold the rice to cover the salmon.

Shape the rice into a triangle.

Place the rice triangle on a sheet of nori.

190

Wrap the nori around the sides like a blanket.

Sprinkle the top point with the sesame seeds.

Or you can wrap the nori over the bottom of the triangle only.

Then sprinkle the other two sides with the sesame seeds.

INGRESO
09:00 hrs

BOLETO DE INGRESO
Llaqta Machupicchu

2303   91211

VALIDO PARA
23/03

PERU

Luis (left) and Miguel (right), our two extremely fun guides, who made sure we didn't get eaten by a caiman in the Amazon.

My friend Megha fell in love with every llama she saw in Peru!

My dad posing in front of Machu Picchu, an ancient Incan city that feels like it sits on the clouds.

I did not know true love until I saw a llama for the first time in Peru. Llamas are like smaller, fluffier, cuter, and more huggable horses. They make very loud, fun noises (look it up on YouTube), and they love to hang out in the mountains of Peru. I mention llamas first because they were basically the mascots of my trip. Anywhere high up, we saw llamas. I considered them my unofficial tour guides. We spent much of our trip to Peru up in the mountains, because that's where a lot of the cool stuff is—like Machu Picchu, an ancient, totally breathtaking Incan city full of intricate and amazingly preserved bridges, sundials, and temples.

Part two of our vacation was a camping trip through the Amazon jungle. I'll get into that more in the rest of this chapter, but it involved caimans (like alligators!), mosquitos, piranhas, two very smiley guides, a scary safety video, and excellent food.

Speaking of food! Peruvian food is awesome. We ate grilled meats and citrusy sauces and even Chinese food—known as chifa, it is the product of Chinese immigrants to Peru. Bonus points if you serve the dishes that follow while doing your best llama impression.

If you want to learn more about the cuisine of Peru, check out these cookbooks:

Peru: The Cookbook by Gastón Acurio
The Fire of Peru: Recipes and Stories from My Peruvian Kitchen by Ricardo Zarate and Jenn Garbee

POLLO A LA BRASA

Serves
4 to 6

I went to Peru as a vegetarian, and I left as a vegetarian who also eats Peruvian-style roasted chicken. Peru is well known for this chicken, which is slow-roasted on a spit over a fire, the natural juices and flavorful marinade seasoning the chicken from the inside out, the crust turning smoky and charred. This is a less traditional, home cook–friendly version of that dish, inspired by the chef Ricardo Zarate's pollo a la brasa recipe in his book, *The Fire of Peru*. His marinade is heavy on ají panca (a fruity, complex-tasting pepper found in Peruvian cooking) and soy sauce, and served with a creamy, herby sauce.

My favorite way to cook this is to put the chicken on a wire rack on the sheet pan and then stick some sliced potatoes and onions underneath it. They'll catch the juices from the chicken and become super delicious. And then you've got dinner and a side!

For the marinade

2 tablespoons store-bought ají panca paste

10 medium garlic cloves, peeled

¼ cup soy sauce

¼ cup red wine vinegar

½ cup olive oil

1½ tablespoons fresh rosemary (no stems!)

1½ teaspoons cumin seeds

1 teaspoon black peppercorns

2 pounds bone-in chicken thighs

For the herb sauce

 1 cup roughly chopped fresh cilantro (stems and leaves)

½ cup mayonnaise

1 teaspoon kosher salt

¾ teaspoon honey or agave

Juice of 1 lime

 TIP
Bone-in chicken thighs have more flavor than boneless.

The crispy, charred edges of the chicken are the best parts!

1   🔪❗ **Make the marinade.** Place the ají panca paste, garlic, soy sauce, vinegar, olive oil, rosemary, cumin seeds, and peppercorns in a blender and blend on high speed until smooth and well incorporated (tiny bits of peppercorn or cumin seed are okay). Use right away or transfer to a covered container and refrigerate for up to 5 days.

2   Put half the marinade and the chicken thighs in a resealable plastic bag. Seal the bag, pressing out all the air, and marinate in the fridge for 12 hours or overnight. (Keep the rest of the marinade in a covered container in the fridge—you'll use it later.)

3   🖐 **Roast the chicken.** Preheat the oven to 425°F. Remove the chicken thighs from the bag with tongs—it's okay if there is still marinade dripping off them—and transfer them to a sheet pan. It's important to use tongs and not touch the chicken with your bare hands. Wash your hands after you complete this step, just to be extra safe, and discard the bag with the used marinade.

4   Put the chicken in the oven and roast for 30 to 45 minutes, until the chicken is sizzling and golden brown. If you have a kitchen thermometer, stick it into the center of a chicken thigh—it should not touch the bone—and make sure it reads at least 165°F. Switch the oven to broil and let the top of the chicken cook until lightly blackened, 2 minutes or so. Remove from the oven, and using a brush or spoon, brush the thighs with the remaining marinade from the container. You don't have to use all of it—just enough so that each piece of chicken is coated.

5   **Make the herb sauce.** While the chicken is roasting, place the cilantro, mayonnaise, salt, honey, and lime juice in the blender and blend on high speed until smooth. Serve alongside the chicken.

SALSA CRIOLLA

Do I have a story for you! When my family went to Peru, we wanted to visit the Amazon rainforest. How hard could it be? The answer: very hard. It rained a lot (I guess the name *rain*forest should have clued us in). We watched a safety video that detailed various disaster scenarios for camping in the Amazon. (Each of the scenarios contained the line "And then . . . things took a turn for the worse.") But under the fearless leadership of our friendly guides, Miguel and Luis, we had the time of our lives. We fished for piranhas, we saw caimans up close, and in the evening, we feasted! Each spread involved salsa criolla, a good-on-everything Peruvian condiment. It's spicy and fresh and tart. Whether we were eating it alongside grilled meat or quinoa soup, it livened up every bite.

Makes about
1½ cups
serving
2 to 4

" Very fun, especially when you eat while you're in the process of cooking it.
—LANDON, 11

½ medium red onion, thinly sliced

2 tablespoons chopped fresh cilantro leaves

8 cherry tomatoes, halved

Juice of ½ lime

1 teaspoon white vinegar

1 Thai chile or serrano pepper, sliced with scissors (optional, or feel free to use just ½ chile; get an adult to help with this and wash your hands after)

¼ teaspoon kosher salt

¼ teaspoon freshly ground black pepper

1 tablespoon olive oil

1 Combine the onion, cilantro, and tomatoes in a small bowl. Add the lime juice, vinegar, chile (if using), salt, and pepper and mix well.

2 Add the olive oil, mix again, and serve immediately or cover and refrigerate until ready to eat.

Peru

KIWICHA PORRIDGE

Serves
2

You've heard me wax on and on about how awesome it was to camp in the Amazon rainforest (if you want to hear more about that, flip to the previous recipe). Nothing set me off on the right foot at the beginning of each day of hiking and fishing like a bowl of kiwicha. Kiwicha, also known as amaranth, is an ancient seed that grows in Peruvian soil and can be eaten like a grain. It soaks up whatever flavors you add to it really well. Every day, I would dress my kiwicha a little differently: sometimes with milk, sugar, and nuts; other times with a heaping scoop of Salsa Criolla (page 199). You can get creative with this—try adding different spices, like cinnamon; sweeteners, like honey or maple syrup; or your favorite condiment. One of my mom's go-to combinations is peanuts, scallions, sesame oil, and soy sauce.

1 cup kiwicha (amaranth)

½ teaspoon kosher salt

For serving

Chopped nuts (I like walnuts)

Maple syrup, brown sugar, or other sweeteners, such as fresh fruit, raisins, chopped dates, or dried figs

Milk

1 Combine 2 cups water and the kiwicha in a medium pot, add the salt, and bring to a boil over high heat. Once you start to see big bubbles in the pot, turn the heat down to medium-low, cover, and cook until the kiwicha is soft and mushy, about 20 minutes. Remove from the heat.

2 Serve the kiwicha in a bowl topped with chopped nuts, your sweeteners of choice, and milk.

TRINIDAD & TOBAGO

On a hike in the jungle with my family! And yes, that is a machete at the bottom of the photo.

We tried to do one of those jumping photos in the water. It wasn't very successful.

knew I would like Tobago when I saw that immediately outside the airport was a bustling convoy of street carts, whose delicious, spice-filled food I could smell from inside the terminal. Trinidad and Tobago—the names of the two islands that make up this Caribbean nation—was a thrilling place to visit for a beach- and food-loving person like myself. We spent days taking long walks along the shore, trying to climb the coconut palms to pick fruit, and then eating even more fruit— and seafood, and rice, and doubles (more on these soon; see the next page). This is a country whose history you can literally see in the food— so many groups, from Indians to West Africans, came through Trinidad and Tobago as forced laborers. They each contributed to the country's cuisine. That's probably why I thought doubles looked so much like the chhole bhature we ate back home; or why ingredients like plantains and okra are commonly found in Trinidadian and Tobagonian food. And then there was the beautiful setting. That beachy air made everything taste even better.

If you want to learn more about the cuisine of Trinidad and Tobago, check out:

Caribbean Flavors for Every Season by Brigid Washington

CURRY CHANA

Serves
4

Everyone loved it. LOVED the cucumber chutney!
—MAYA, 8

Doubles are a classic Trinidadian food that starts with two layers of bara, or fried dough, that are then filled with curry chana. In Tobago, a local told us that this white van parks outside a clothing shop around lunchtime and sells doubles. We showed up and, miraculously, the van came! The bara was stretchy and yummy, and the curry chana was like eating chickpeas in Technicolor. The family of my friend the cookbook author Brigid Washington hails from Trinidad and Tobago, and one of her favorite dishes to make for her family is this curry chana. She often eats it with rice instead of sandwiching it in bara because deep-frying bread at home is challenging. This is Brigid's recipe, which she serves with a refreshing and crunchy cucumber chutney. And if you want to try the real deal with the bara, go for it, and please mail me a few pieces while you're at it.

For the chana

2 tablespoons vegetable oil

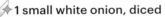
1 small white onion, diced

8 garlic cloves, crushed (the bottom of a can works well for this)

1 tablespoon Madras curry powder

2 (15-ounce) cans chickpeas, drained and rinsed

5 large scallions, sliced

8 cilantro sprigs, chopped

1 teaspoon kosher salt

1 teaspoon freshly ground black pepper

Hot sauce, such as Tapatío, Frank's RedHot, or Cholula (optional)

For the cucumber chutney

1 large English cucumber, grated (about 1 cup)

4 garlic cloves, minced

6 cilantro sprigs, chopped

½ teaspoon kosher salt

Juice of 1 lime

Cooked rice and/or bara, for serving

1 **Make the chana.** Warm the oil in a large skillet over medium-high heat. Once it's hot, add the onions and garlic and cook, stirring occasionally, until soft, 5 to 7 minutes. Stir in the curry powder and then add ½ cup water.

2 Stir in the chickpeas, scallions, cilantro, salt, and pepper. Turn the heat down to medium-low, add 1 more cup water, and simmer until the chickpeas are tender, 15 to 20 minutes, adding more water, ¼ cup at a time, if the mixture starts to look dry. Use a potato masher or the back of a spoon to mash some of the chickpeas. Add hot sauce to taste, a few dashes at a time, if you like it spicy!

3 **Make the chutney.** Mix together the cucumber, garlic, cilantro, salt, and lime juice in a small bowl. Refrigerate until needed.

4 Serve the chickpeas with the chutney, alongside rice and/or bara. This tastes even better as leftovers, when the chickpeas have had a chance to really deepen in flavor!

STEWED FISH

You know how certain dishes just perfume the kitchen with irresistible smells and make you impatient to eat? This stewed fish is like that. We were lucky enough to get a taste of home cooking when we visited Tobago, and I'll never forget how hungry I got just sitting in the living room, wondering what was being prepared in the next room. This stewed fish is hearty and tangy, overflowing with flavor from the herb-filled green seasoning. The recipe was developed by my friend Brigid, and she says that whenever she was having a bad day, her mom somehow knew to make this dish.

Serves

4

"LOVED the fish once it was fried.
—MAYA, 8

For the green seasoning

 1 small yellow onion, roughly chopped

6 garlic cloves, peeled

4 scallions, chopped

½ bunch fresh parsley (stems and leaves), roughly chopped (about ½ cup)

½ bunch fresh cilantro (stems and leaves), roughly chopped (about ½ cup)

½ habanero or Thai chile, seeds removed, sliced with scissors (optional; get an adult to help with this and wash your hands after)

For the fish

1 teaspoon kosher salt

1 teaspoon freshly ground black pepper

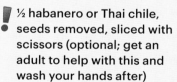 Zest and juice of 2 limes (get an adult to help you use a zester!)

½ teaspoon paprika

2 pounds mackerel, swordfish, or cod fillets (mackerel will be the most fishy, and cod will be the least fishy; have the fish deboned and cut into individual servings at the grocery store)

½ cup all-purpose flour

1 teaspoon garlic powder

¼ cup vegetable oil

For the stew

2 tablespoons vegetable oil

6 garlic cloves, crushed (the bottom of a can works well for this)

½ small yellow onion, sliced

2 tablespoons fresh thyme

2 tablespoons minced fresh ginger

4 scallions, sliced

TIP
You'll have some down time while the fish is marinating. That's a great opportunity to cut all the vegetables for the stew.

4 Roma tomatoes, diced

2 tablespoons ketchup

1 tablespoon soy sauce

1 tablespoon fish sauce

1 tablespoon light brown sugar

1 green bell pepper, stem and seeds removed, thinly sliced

1 red bell pepper, stem and seeds removed, thinly sliced

Cooked rice, for serving

Trinidad & Tobago

1 **Make the green seasoning.** Place the onion, garlic, scallions, parsley, cilantro, and chile (if using) in a blender or a food processor and blend into a puree (with an adult to supervise). You should still be able to see bits of onion and garlic.

2 **Prepare the fish.** Mix ¼ cup of the green seasoning with ½ teaspoon of the salt, ½ teaspoon of the pepper, the lime zest, lime juice, and paprika. Use a spoon or a brush to spread that mixture over all sides of the fish fillets. Put the fish on a plate or in a shallow bowl, cover with plastic wrap or a lid, and let marinate in the refrigerator for 20 minutes, or up to an hour. Wash your hands after handling the fish! Store the rest of the green seasoning for a later use—as a marinade, mixed with olive oil to make a dip, or as a condiment!

3 While the fish is marinating, prepare your coating for the fish by combining the flour, remaining ½ teaspoon salt, remaining ½ teaspoon pepper, and the garlic powder on a large plate. One at a time, place a fish fillet on the plate, flipping it to coat all sides in the flour mixture. Repeat with all the fillets.

4 Warm the oil in a large, deep skillet over medium-high heat for 2 minutes. Put a plate lined with a few paper towels next to the stove.

5 When the oil starts to shimmer (test the oil by sprinkling a little flour into the skillet; if it sizzles, the oil is ready), place the floured fish in the skillet and cook until each side is a medium golden color and the fish feels firm when you poke it, 3 to 4 minutes per side.* Ask an adult to help with this step, as the oil can splatter. Also, do not overcrowd the pan in this step; cook the fish in batches if necessary.

*If you're not quite ready to pan-fry, and the above step feels too tough for you, you can skip it entirely (though Brigid, the author of this recipe, says it does add quite a bit of flavor and texture!). If you don't want to fry, don't coat the fish fillets in flour. You may need to cook them a little longer in the next step, though.

recipe continues →

Trinidad & Tobago

6 Using kitchen tongs or a spatula, carefully place the cooked fish on the paper towel–lined plate. Let the skillet cool down, and then wipe it out with a paper towel.

7 **Make the stew.** Add the 2 tablespoons of oil to the same skillet, set it over medium heat, then add the garlic, onions, thyme, and ginger and cook, stirring, until soft and fragrant, about 2 minutes. Add the scallions, tomatoes, ketchup, soy sauce, fish sauce, brown sugar, and 1½ cups water and stir to combine.

8 Gently return the fish to the pan (or if you skipped the frying step, add it now), and nestle each fillet into this aromatic mixture. Turn the heat down to medium-low, cover the pan with a lid, and simmer until the fish has absorbed some of the stew and resembles the color of the sauce, 10 to 12 minutes. The sauce will also thicken up a bit.

9 Add the bell peppers, cover the pan with a lid, and simmer until the peppers are soft but still a little firm, another 5 to 10 minutes.

10 Serve over rice.

Mix the seasonings for the fish.

Spoon the paste over the fish and let marinate.

Coat the fish in the flour mixture.

Fry the fish.

Cook until golden and firm on both sides, then remove the fish from the pan.

In the same skillet, make the sauce, return the fish to the stew, then add the vegetables.

ACKNOWLEDGMENTS

I owe so much to my amazing recipe testers, all kids just like you! Thank you to these outstanding cooks:

Te, 6	Madisen, 9	Axel, 5	Ishaan, 8
Beatrix, 10	Blaine, 9	Milo, 6	Shivani, 10
Ethan, 9	Lucas, 10	Nina, 3	Nayan, 12
Landon, 11	Madeline, 5	Ashiyana, 6	Noémie, 9
Ishan, 9	Zoë, 9	Kai, 9	Radhika, 11
Penny, 9	Riley, 7	Maya, 8	
Julia, 13	Alex, 7	Niko, 5	
Evelyn, 11	Nora, 13	Finn, 7½	

Thanks to my agent, **Sarah Smith,** for making my dream to write a more inclusive kids' cookbook come true, and to **Stephanie Fletcher** and the team at Harvest for matching my enthusiasm for approaching this book with fun, creativity, and a little weirdness. My friends are the best and listened to me as I talked endlessly through all my ideas for this book and fretted about getting it done on time. Special shout-outs to **Lauren Vespoli, Kate Taylor, Kelly Tropin, James Lee, Khushbu Shah, Sonia Chopra,** and **Tejal Rao.** Thanks to my sister and brother-in-law, **Meera Krishna** and **David Peterson,** who have been amazingly supportive and whose strength inspires me beyond belief. Thanks also to my amazing relatives and their children, whose opinions were instrumental in making sure this book spoke directly to awesome kids like you! To the talented and generous people behind so many of the recipes in this book: **Helen and Billie Bitzas, Namiko Chen, Shanti Dev, Ham El-Waylly, Tatiana Gupta, Mourad Lahlou, Rick Martínez, Hetty McKinnon, Ijaz Parpia, Brigid Washington, Ricardo Zarate.** And to the fabulous photography team who brought to life my kitchen adventures and became a part of our little Dallas family for two weeks: **Mackenzie Smith Kelley, Maite Aizpurua, Mary McNally,** and **Ayesha Erkin.**

An extra special thank-you to the **Singhal family. Radhika** and **Rishika,** you were the best hand models. **Anupam Mama** and **Neha Mami,** thank you for bringing your kids to our house and letting them eat all of the sugar!

Seth Byrum: I still can't believe I married The Guy. I love you so much.

And finally to my parents, **Ritu and Shailendra Krishna.** I am who I am because of you, and I wouldn't trade that for anything. Thank you for showing me the world, and for believing that I could make a whole job out of eating for a living.

Note: Page references in *italics* indicate recipe photographs.

A

adult assistance, xvii
Agua Fresca, Watermelon, 36, *37*
Apples
    Tarte aux Pommes, 54–61, *55*
Artichokes with Butter, *42*, 43–44

B

Baklava, 17–19
Bao
    Chocolate Buns, 86
    Dou Sha Bao, 83–89, *84*
Basil
    Caprese Salad, *116*, 117
    Pesto Pasta, 120, *121*
Beans
    Curry Chana, 206–8, *207*
    Dahi Bhalla, Nana Style,
        160–63, *161*
    Dou Sha Bao, 83–89, *84*
    Ful Medames, 96–97, *97*
    Hummus bi Tehina, 94–95
    Koshari, 98–101, *99*
    Mom's Ribollita, 122–23
    "Pickled" and Stir-Fried Long
        Beans with Pork,
        73–75, *74*
    Tostadas with Refried Beans
        and Squash, 30–33,
        31–32
    Vegetable Tagine, 135–36, *137*

Beef
    Hot Pot, 76–80, *77*
Bell peppers
    Bell Pepper and Cheese
        Quesadillas, 34–35
    Chicken Meatballs, 175–76
    Sheet-Pan Panzanella, 106–8,
        107
    slicing and dicing, xix
    Stewed Fish, 209–13, *210*
Bento Boxes, *172*, 173–74
Bread
    Dad's English Breakfast,
        144–45, *145*
    Mom's Ribollita, 122–23
    Shahi Toast, 164–65
    Sheet-Pan Panzanella, 106–8,
        107
Briam, 9–10, *11*

C

Cabbage
    Hot Pot, 76–80, *77*
Caprese Salad, *116*, 117
Carrots
    Vegetable Tagine, 135–36,
        137
Cheese
    Bell Pepper and Cheese
        Quesadillas, 34–35
    Caprese Salad, *116*, 117

    Cucumber Tea Sandwiches
        with Cream Cheese, 147
    Elotes, 24–26, *25*
    Pear and Gorgonzola Ravioli,
        109–15, *110*
    Quiche Lorraine, 49–50, *50*
    Spanakopita, *4*, 5–7
    Tiramisu, 124–27, *125*
    Tostadas with Refried Beans
        and Squash, 30–33,
        31–32
    Zaalouk with Halloumi, *132*,
        133–34
Chicken
    Chicken Meatballs, 175–76
    Hot Pot, 76–80, *77*
    Pollo a la Brasa, 196–98, *197*
    Pozole Verde con Pollo,
        27–29, *28*
Chickpeas
    Curry Chana, 206–8, *207*
    Dahi Bhalla, Nana Style,
        160–63, *161*
    Hummus bi Tehina, 94–95
    Koshari, 98–101, *99*
    Vegetable Tagine, 135–36,
        137
Chiles
    Daqqa, 98–101, *99*
    Pozole Verde con Pollo,
        27–29, *28*
    Salsa Criolla, 199

Chiles (*cont.*)
  slicing, xviii
  Stewed Fish, 209–13, *210*
China, 65–72
  cookbooks, 67
  Dou Sha Bao, 83–89, *84*
  Fried Rice, 81–82
  Hot Pot, 76–80, *77*
  "Pickled" and Stir-Fried Long
    Beans with Pork,
    73–75, *74*
  Pork and Chive Dumplings, *68*,
    69–72
  sightseeing, 66–67
Chive and Pork Dumplings, *68*,
  69–72
Chocolate
  Chocolate Buns, 86
  Mousse au Chocolat, 51–53, *52*
  Shortcut Profiteroles,
    62–63, *63*
  Tiramisu, 124–27, *125*
Chutney, Cucumber, 206–8, *207*
Cilantro
  Pollo a la Brasa, 196–98, *197*
  Stewed Fish, 209–13, *210*
Coffee
  Tiramisu, 124–27, *125*
Corn and hominy
  Elotes, 24–26, *25*
  Pozole Verde con Pollo,
    27–29, *28*
Couscous, *137*, 138
Crepes, 46–48, *47*
Cucumbers
  Cucumber Chutney, 206–8,
    207
  Cucumber Tea Sandwiches
    with Cream Cheese, 147
  cutting, xix
  Sheet-Pan Panzanella, 106–8,
    107
  Traditional Cucumber Tea
    Sandwiches, 146
  Tzatziki, 8

Curry
  Curry Chana, 206–8, *207*
  Palakkad Shrimp Curry, *156*,
    157–59

D

Dad's English Breakfast, 144–45,
  145
Dahi Bhalla, Nana Style, 160–63,
  161
Daqqa, 98–101, *99*
Desserts
  Baklava, 17–19
  Chocolate Buns, 86
  Dou Sha Bao, 83–89, *84*
  Mousse au Chocolat,
    51–53, *52*
  Shortcut Profiteroles,
    62–63, *63*
  Tarte aux Pommes, 54–61, *55*
  Tiramisu, 124–27, *125*
Dipping Sauce, 79
Dips
  Ful Medames, 96–97, *97*
  Hummus bi Tehina, 94–95
  Tzatziki, 8
Dolmades, *12*, 13–16
Dou Sha Bao, 83–89, *84*
Drinks
  Moroccan Mint Tea, 139
  Salty or Sweet Lassi, 166–67
  Watermelon Agua Fresca,
    36, *37*
Dumplings, Pork and Chive, *68*,
  69–72

E

Eggplant
  cutting, xix
  Zaalouk with Halloumi, *132*,
    133–34
Eggs
  Fried Rice, 81–82

Life-Changing Udon with
    Soft-Boiled Egg, Hot Soy
    Sauce, and Black Pepper,
    177–79, *178*
  Quiche Lorraine, 49–50, *50*
Egypt, 91–101
  cookbook, 93
  Ful Medames, 96–97, *97*
  Hummus bi Tehina, 94–95
  Koshari, 98–101, *99*
  sightseeing, 92–93
Elotes, 24–26, *25*
England, 141–51
  cookbooks, 143
  Dad's English Breakfast,
    144–45, *145*
  Scones, 148–51, *149*
  sightseeing, 142–43
  Tea Sandwiches, 146–47

F

Fish
  Salmon Onigiri, 187–91, *191*
  Smoked Salmon Tea
    Sandwiches with Herb
    Butter, 147
  Stewed Fish, 209–13, *210*
France, 39–63
  Artichokes with Butter, *42*,
    43–44
  cookbooks, 41
  Crepes, 46–48, *47*
  Gratin Dauphinois, 45
  Mousse au Chocolat,
    51–53, *52*
  Quiche Lorraine, 49–50, *50*
  Shortcut Profiteroles,
    62–63, *63*
  sightseeing, 40–41
  Tarte aux Pommes, 54–61, *55*
Fried Rice, 81–82
Fruits. See also specific fruits
  washing, xvi
Ful Medames, 96–97, *97*

G

Garlic, crushing, xviii
Ginger, preparing, xix
Grape leaves
  Dolmades, *12*, 13–16
Gratin Dauphinois, 45
Greece, 1–19
  Baklava, 17–19
  Briam, 9–10, *11*
  cookbooks, 3
  Dolmades, *12*, 13–16
  sightseeing, 2–3
  Spanakopita, *4*, 5–7
  Tzatziki, 8

H

Ham
  Quiche Lorraine, 49–50, *50*
Herbs
  Caprese Salad, *116*, 117
  Dolmades, *12*, 13–16
  Moroccan Mint Tea, 139
  Pesto Pasta, 120, *121*
  Pollo a la Brasa, 196–98, *197*
  Smoked Salmon Tea
    Sandwiches with Herb
    Butter, 147
  Stewed Fish, 209–13, *210*
  Zaalouk with Halloumi, *132*,
    133–34
Hominy
  Pozole Verde con Pollo,
    27–29, *28*
Honey
  Baklava, 17–19
Hot Pot, 76–80, *77*
How to Bento!, *172*, 173–74
Hummus bi Tehina, 94–95

I

Ice cream
  Shortcut Profiteroles,
    62–63, *63*

India, 153–67
  cookbooks, 155
  Dahi Bhalla, Nana Style,
    160–63, *161*
  Palakkad Shrimp Curry, *156*,
    157–59
  Salty or Sweet Lassi, 166–67
  Shahi Toast, 164–65
  sightseeing, 154–55
Italy, 103–8
  Caprese Salad, *116*, 117
  cookbook, 105
  Mom's Ribollita, 122–23
  Pear and Gorgonzola Ravioli,
    109–15, *110*
  Penne Arrabbiata, 118–19
  Pesto Pasta, 120, *121*
  Sheet-Pan Panzanella, 106–8,
    107
  sightseeing, 104–5
  Tiramisu, 124–27, *125*

J

Japan, 169–91
  Chicken Meatballs, 175–76
  cookbooks, 171
  How to Bento!, *172*, 173–74
  Life-Changing Udon with
    Soft-Boiled Egg, Hot Soy
    Sauce, and Black Pepper,
    177–79, *178*
  Miso Ramen, 184–86, *185*
  Salmon Onigiri, 187–91, *191*
  sightseeing, 170–71
  Soba with Peanut Sauce, 183
  Zaru Soba, 180–83, *181*

K

Katsuobushi
  Zaru Soba, 180–83, *181*
kitchen setup, xvi
Kiwicha Porridge, 200, *201*
knife advice, xviii
Koshari, 98–101, *99*

L

Ladyfinger cookies
  Tiramisu, 124–27, *125*
Lassi, Salty or Sweet, 166–67
Lentils
  Koshari, 98–101, *99*
Life-Changing Udon with Soft-
  Boiled Egg, Hot Soy
  Sauce, and Black Pepper,
  177–79, *178*
Long Beans, "Pickled" and Stir-
  Fried, with Pork,
  73–75, *74*

M

measurements, xvii
Meat. *See also* Ham; Pork
  handling safely, xvi
  Hot Pot, 76–80, *77*
Meatballs, Chicken, 175–76
Mexico, 21–37
  Bell Pepper and Cheese
    Quesadillas, 34–35
  cookbooks, 23
  Elotes, 24–26, *25*
  Pozole Verde con Pollo,
    27–29, *28*
  sightseeing, 22–23
  Tostadas with Refried Beans
    and Squash, 30–33,
    31–32
  Watermelon Agua Fresca,
    36, *37*
Mint Tea, Moroccan, 139
Miso Ramen, 184–86, *185*
Mom's Ribollita, 122–23
Morocco, 129–39
  cookbooks, 131
  Couscous, *137*, 138
  Moroccan Mint Tea, 139
  sightseeing, 130–31
  Vegetable Tagine, 135–36, *137*
  Zaalouk with Halloumi, *132*,
    133–34

Mousse au Chocolat, 51–53, *52*
Mushrooms
    Hot Pot, 76–80, *77*

N

Noodles
    Hot Pot, 76–80, *77*
    Life-Changing Udon with
        Soft-Boiled Egg, Hot Soy
        Sauce, and Black Pepper,
        177–79, *178*
    Miso Ramen, 184–86, *185*
    Soba with Peanut Sauce,
        183
    Zaru Soba, 180–83, *181*
Nori
    Salmon Onigiri, 187–91, *191*
Nuts
    Baklava, 17–19
    Shahi Toast, 164–65

O

Olives
    Briam, 9–10, *11*
    Sheet-Pan Panzanella, 106–8,
        107
    Vegetable Tagine, 135–36,
        137
Onigiri, Salmon, 187–91, *191*
Onions, cutting, xix

P

Palakkad Shrimp Curry, *156*,
    157–59
Panzanella, Sheet-Pan, 106–8,
    107
Pasta
    Couscous, *137*, 138
    Koshari, 98–101, *99*
    Pear and Gorgonzola Ravioli,
        109–15, *110*
    Penne Arrabbiata, 118–19
    Pesto Pasta, 120, *121*

Peanut butter
    Dipping Sauce, 79
    Soba with Peanut Sauce, 183
Pear and Gorgonzola Ravioli,
    109–15, *110*
Penne Arrabbiata, 118–19
Peppers. *See* Bell peppers; Chiles
Peru, 193–201
    cookbooks, 195
    Kiwicha Porridge, 200, *201*
    Pollo a la Brasa, 196–98, *197*
    Salsa Criolla, 199
    sightseeing, 194–95
Pesto Pasta, 120, *121*
Phyllo dough
    Baklava, 17–19
    Spanakopita, *4*, 5–7
"Pickled" and Stir-Fried Long
        Beans with Pork,
        73–75, *74*
Pistachios
    Baklava, 17–19
    Shahi Toast, 164–65
Pollo a la Brasa, 196–98, *197*
Pork
    Hot Pot, 76–80, *77*
    Miso Ramen, 184–86, *185*
    "Pickled" and Stir-Fried Long
        Beans with Pork,
        73–75, *74*
    Pork and Chive Dumplings, *68*,
        69–72
    Quiche Lorraine, 49–50, *50*
Porridge, Kiwicha, 200, *201*
Potatoes
    Briam, 9–10, *11*
    cutting, xviii
    Dad's English Breakfast,
        144–45, *145*
    Dahi Bhalla, Nana Style,
        160–63, *161*
    Gratin Dauphinois, 45
    Vegetable Tagine, 135–36, *137*
Pozole Verde con Pollo,
    27–29, *28*
Profiteroles, Shortcut, 62–63, *63*

Q

Quesadillas, Bell Pepper and
    Cheese, 34–35
Quiche Lorraine, 49–50, *50*

R

Ramen, Miso, 184–86, *185*
Ravioli, Pear and Gorgonzola,
    109–15, *110*
recipe tips
    be organized, xvi
    keep an open mind, xvii
    keep things clean, xvi
    read the recipe ahead, xvi
    taste as you go, xvii
    understand measurements,
        xvii
    vegetable cutting guide,
        xviii–xix
    watch for symbols, xvii
Red bean paste
    Dou Sha Bao, 83–89, *84*
Ribollita, Mom's, 122–23
Rice
    Dolmades, *12*, 13–16
    Fried Rice, 81–82
    Koshari, 98–101, *99*
    Salmon Onigiri, 187–91, *191*

S

Salad, Caprese, *116*, 117
Salmon
    Salmon Onigiri, 187–91, *191*
    Smoked Salmon Tea
        Sandwiches with Herb
        Butter, 147
Salsa Criolla, 199
Salty or Sweet Lassi, 166–67
Sandwiches
    Cucumber Tea Sandwiches
        with Cream Cheese, 147
    Smoked Salmon Tea
        Sandwiches with Herb
        Butter, 147

Traditional Cucumber Tea
    Sandwiches, 146
Sauces
    Dipping Sauce, 79
    Salsa Criolla, 199
    Tzatziki, 8
Scallions, cutting, xviii
Scones, 148–51, *149*
Shahi Toast, 164–65
Sheet-Pan Panzanella, 106–8,
    107
Shellfish. *See* Shrimp
Shortcut Profiteroles, 62–63, *63*
Shrimp
    Hot Pot, 76–80, *77*
    Palakkad Shrimp Curry, *156*,
        157–59
Smoked Salmon Tea Sandwiches
    with Herb Butter, 147
Soba
    Soba with Peanut Sauce, 183
    Zaru Soba, 180–83, *181*
Soup. *See* Ribollita
Spanakopita, *4*, 5–7
Spinach
    Hot Pot, 76–80, *77*
    Spanakopita, *4*, 5–7
Squash
    Briam, 9–10, *11*
    cutting zucchini, xix
    Mom's Ribollita, 122–23
    Tostadas with Refried Beans
        and Squash, 30–33,
        31–32
    Vegetable Tagine, 135–36, *137*
Stews
    Pozole Verde con Pollo,
        27–29, *28*
    Stewed Fish, 209–13, *210*
    Vegetable Tagine, 135–36, *137*

Tagine, Vegetable, 135–36,
    137
Tahini
    Dipping Sauce, 79
    Hummus bi Tehina, 94–95
Tarte aux Pommes, 54–61, *55*
Tasting before serving, xvii
Tea, Moroccan Mint, 139
Tea Sandwiches, 146–47
Tiramisu, 124–27, *125*
Toast, Shahi, 164–65
Tofu
    Chicken Meatballs, 175–76
    Hot Pot, 76–80, *77*
Tomatoes
    Briam, 9–10, *11*
    Caprese Salad, *116*, 117
    Dad's English Breakfast,
        144–45, *145*
    Koshari, 98–101, *99*
    Mom's Ribollita, 122–23
    Penne Arrabbiata, 118–19
    Salsa Criolla, 199
    Sheet-Pan Panzanella, 106–8,
        107
    Zaalouk with Halloumi, *132*,
        133–34
Tortillas. *See* Quesadillas
Tostadas with Refried Beans
    and Squash, 30–33,
        31–32
Traditional Cucumber Tea
    Sandwiches, 146
Trinidad & Tobago, 203–13
    cookbook, 205
    Curry Chana, 206–8, *207*
    sightseeing, 204–5
    Stewed Fish, 209–13, *210*
Tzatziki, 8

Udon, Life-Changing, with
    Soft-Boiled Egg, Hot Soy
    Sauce, and Black Pepper,
    177–79, *178*

Vegetables. See also specific
    vegetables
    cutting guide, xviii–xix
    Fried Rice, 81–82
    Hot Pot, 76–80, *77*
    Soba with Peanut Sauce, 183
    Vegetable Tagine, 135–36, *137*
    washing, xvi

Walnuts
    Baklava, 17–19
Watermelon Agua Fresca, 36, *37*

Yogurt
    Dahi Bhalla, Nana Style,
        160–63, *161*
    Salty or Sweet Lassi, 166–67
    Tzatziki, 8

Zaalouk with Halloumi, *132*,
    133–34
Zaru Soba, 180–83, *181*
Zucchini
    Briam, 9–10, *11*
    cutting, xix
    Mom's Ribollita, 122–23

T

U

V

W

Y

Z

PRIYA KRISHNA is a food reporter and video host for the *New York Times* and the *New York Times* bestselling author of multiple cookbooks, including *Indian-ish* and *Cooking at Home*. Her stories have been included in the 2019 and 2021 editions of *The Best American Food Writing,* she has been nominated for James Beard and IACP awards, and in 2021, she was named to *Forbes's* 30 Under 30 list. She is originally from Dallas, Texas, which happens to be one of the busiest travel hubs in the world.

DESIGN YOUR OWN PASSPORT